Mastering Time - Innovative Solutions to Complex Scheduling Problems

Edited by Ali Soofastaei

Published in London, United Kingdom

Mastering Time - Innovative Solutions to Complex Scheduling Problems
http://dx.doi.org/10.5772/intechopen.1003431
Edited by Ali Soofastaei

Contributors
A. Madhumitha, Ali Soofastaei, Cristina-Sorina Stângaciu, E. Saranya, G. Rajeshkumar, Hafed Motair, K. Saranya, Krisztián Attila Bakon, Petar Przulj, Peter Moo, R. Kavitha, S. Sriram, Zhen Ding, Zhen Qu

First published in London, United Kingdom, 2025 by IntechOpen
IntechOpen is the global imprint of INTECHOPEN LIMITED, registered in England and Wales, registration number: 11086078, 167-169 Great Portland Street, London, W1W 5PF, United Kingdom

For EU product safety concerns: IN TECH d.o.o., Prolaz Marije Krucifikse Kozulić 3, 51000 Rijeka, Croatia, info@intechopen.com or visit our website at intechopen.com.

British Library Cataloguing-in-Publication Data
A catalogue record for this book is available from the British Library

Mastering Time - Innovative Solutions to Complex Scheduling Problems
Edited by Ali Soofastaei
p. cm.
Print ISBN 978-1-83769-428-0
Online ISBN 978-1-83769-427-3
eBook (PDF) ISBN 978-1-83769-429-7

If disposing of this product, please recycle the paper responsibly.

Meet the editor

Dr. Ali Soofastaei is a global leader in artificial intelligence (AI) projects, an international keynote speaker, and a professional author. He completed his Ph.D. and was a Postdoctoral Research Fellow at the University of Queensland in Australia, where he studied AI applications in mining engineering. As a scientific supervisor, he has provided practical guidance to mechanical and mining engineering and information technology students for many years. Dr. Soofastaei has more than fifteen years of academic experience as an Assistant Professor and leader of global research activities. Results from his research and development projects have been published in international journals and keynote presentations. He has been involved in industrial research and development projects in several industries, including oil and gas, steel, and mining.

Contents

Preface

Time management and scheduling have long been recognized as critical factors in achieving industry efficiency and productivity. The ability to allocate limited resources—whether human, material, or computational—against competing demands optimally is a fundamental challenge organizations and individuals face. Scheduling problems, in their many forms, are deeply intertwined with operational research, artificial intelligence, and decision science, making them a topic of continuous study and innovation.

This volume, *Mastering Time – Innovative Solutions to Complex Scheduling Problems*, presents a comprehensive exploration of modern scheduling challenges and the methodologies employed to address them. It aims to bridge the gap between theoretical advancements and practical applications, offering a multidisciplinary perspective on how scheduling can be optimized in an era of rapid technological change. By bringing together concepts from mathematics, computer science, engineering, and business analytics, this book provides a holistic view of how scheduling solutions can be designed, implemented, and refined to meet the demands of complex systems.

Scope and objectives

The primary objective of this book is to present state-of-the-art strategies and methodologies for solving scheduling problems across various domains. From industrial operations to healthcare systems, from workforce management to supply chain logistics, scheduling is an essential function that impacts efficiency, cost-effectiveness, and overall system performance. By exploring algorithmic approaches, machine learning techniques, and heuristic optimization strategies, this volume offers readers a structured understanding of both foundational theories and cutting-edge developments in scheduling.

In particular, the book focuses on:

- Theoretical frameworks that underpin scheduling and time management.
- Optimization techniques, including linear programming, integer programming, and constraint-based scheduling.
- The role of artificial intelligence and machine learning in predictive scheduling and automation.
- Case studies from industries such as mining, manufacturing, healthcare, transportation, and technology illustrate real-world scheduling model applications.
- Challenges and solutions in dynamic scheduling, including uncertainty management, real-time decision-making, and adaptive scheduling frameworks.
- The intersection of scheduling with data governance, digital twins, and cloud-based computing environments.

The book is structured to provide both conceptual depth and practical relevance, making it accessible to researchers, practitioners, and decision-makers. The content is designed to assist professionals in improving scheduling efficiency while equipping scholars with an academic foundation for further research in this field.

Target audience

This book is intended for a diverse audience, including researchers, graduate students, industry professionals, and policymakers involved in operations management, artificial intelligence, and decision sciences. Engineers and data scientists working on real-world scheduling problems will find valuable insights into advanced methodologies, while business leaders and executives will gain a strategic understanding of how scheduling optimization can drive operational excellence.

For academics, this volume serves as a resource for understanding the mathematical and algorithmic scheduling principles, offering insights into the latest advancements in computational approaches. For industry practitioners, the book provides practical strategies that can be applied to improve scheduling efficiency and adaptability within complex operational environments.

Acknowledgements

The development of this volume has been a collaborative effort, and I want to express my deep appreciation to all those who contributed to its realization. I extend my gratitude to the researchers, industry experts, and scholars whose insights and contributions have enriched this book. Their expertise has played a crucial role in shaping the discussions presented here.

I also want to acknowledge the support of my colleagues and peers, who have provided valuable feedback throughout the editorial process. Their perspectives and constructive critiques have significantly enhanced the clarity and relevance of the content. Additionally, I am grateful to the editorial and publishing teams whose diligence and professionalism have facilitated the completion of this work.

Conclusion

As industries and societies evolve in an increasingly data-driven and technology-enabled world, scheduling will remain paramount in optimizing efficiency and decision-making. Organizations can achieve greater resilience, productivity, and strategic advantage by mastering scheduling techniques. I hope that *Mastering Time – Innovative Solutions to Complex Scheduling Problems* will serve as both a scholarly reference and a practical guide for those seeking to tackle the complexities of scheduling with innovation and precision.

Ali Soofastaei
CEO,
Innovative Artificial Intelligence,
Brisbane, Australia

Chapter 1

Introductory Chapter: Mastering Time – Innovative Solutions to Complex Scheduling Problems

Ali Soofastaei

1. Introduction

Time is both an infinite and a finite resource. While it continues its relentless march forward, our ability to utilize it efficiently is limited by our understanding, tools, and approaches. In the modern world, where industries and individuals constantly strive for optimization, mastering time has become a critical factor in achieving success. From large-scale industrial operations to personal time management, the challenge of scheduling—the process of organizing tasks, events, or resources within given constraints—remains one of the most complex yet essential aspects of modern life [1].

At the heart of scheduling lies a fundamental question: How can we best allocate our most valuable resource, time, in a world of competing demands? The answer is far from straightforward. Scheduling involves coordinating multiple tasks and events, often with conflicting priorities, limited resources, and unpredictable changes. Whether it is a manufacturing plant operating 24/7, a healthcare system managing patient appointments, or an individual juggling work, family, and personal commitments, effective scheduling is central to achieving objectives with minimal waste and maximum efficiency [2].

Despite its critical importance, scheduling is often overlooked or oversimplified in many contexts. People and organizations tend to rely on intuition or outdated methods, unaware of the complexities and inefficiencies that may be creeping into their processes. However, modern scheduling problems require sophisticated solutions, ones that not only optimize the use of time but also manage resources, minimize costs, and adapt to changing conditions. This book is a roadmap for navigating those complexities and unlocking the full potential of time and resource management.

2. The complexity of scheduling problems

Scheduling problems are, by nature, multi-dimensional and complex. They are not just about placing tasks on a timeline but involve managing constraints such as resource availability, task dependencies, and time windows. In more technical terms, scheduling is a combinatorial optimization problem—one where finding the best solution often requires considering a multitude of possible scenarios.

For instance, take the case of a large-scale construction project where multiple teams must coordinate their efforts. Delays in one area can cascade into others, causing costly overruns. Or consider a hospital managing the schedules of doctors, nurses, and patients. Missteps in scheduling can result in both inefficiencies and, more critically, risks to patient care. In such situations, the stakes are high, and the complexity of scheduling increases exponentially as more variables are introduced [3].

The complexity of scheduling arises from several factors:

1. *Multiple resources*: In most scheduling problems, there are multiple resources that need to be coordinated, such as personnel, equipment, or materials. Each resource may have different availability and capacity constraints. For example, in manufacturing, machines may have different processing speeds and maintenance requirements, while in health care, doctors and nurses have varying expertise and work shifts.

2. *Dependencies and precedence*: Many tasks cannot be completed in isolation. They are dependent on the completion of other tasks, often in a specific order. For instance, in construction, foundations must be laid before walls can be built. In project management, certain milestones must be achieved before subsequent tasks can begin. These dependencies create a network of interrelated tasks that must be carefully coordinated.

3. *Time-sensitive constraints*: Some tasks must be completed within specific time windows or deadlines. Missing these windows can lead to penalties, missed opportunities, or even project failure. In industries like transportation and logistics, where schedules are tightly linked to delivery times, delays can have far-reaching consequences.

4. *Dynamic and uncertain environments*: Scheduling is often complicated by the fact that real-world environments are dynamic and unpredictable. Unforeseen disruptions, such as equipment breakdowns, resource shortages, or changing customer demands, can force schedules to be re-adjusted on the fly. This adds another layer of complexity, as the scheduling system must be flexible enough to adapt in real time.

5. *Multiple objectives*: Most scheduling problems are multi-objective. In addition to minimizing time, decision-makers may need to optimize other factors, such as costs, resource utilization, quality, or customer satisfaction. Balancing these objectives requires careful trade-offs and strategic prioritization.

3. Traditional vs. modern scheduling approaches

Traditional methods of managing schedules, while effective in some contexts, are increasingly ill-suited to the demands of modern industries and personal lives. For many years, tools like spreadsheets and basic project management software were sufficient for handling schedules, particularly in smaller operations with fewer constraints. However, as the complexity of operations has grown, these methods have shown their limitations [4].

In industries like manufacturing, health care, and logistics, where multiple tasks, resources, and time-sensitive constraints intersect, traditional tools are often too rigid and simplistic. They lack the ability to dynamically adjust to changing circumstances, leading to inefficiencies, delays, and missed opportunities. Moreover, manual scheduling is not only time-consuming but also prone to human error, especially when dealing with complex systems [5].

This is where modern approaches to scheduling come into play. In recent years, there has been a surge of interest in using advanced technologies such as artificial intelligence (AI), machine learning, and optimization algorithms to solve scheduling problems more effectively. These tools are designed to handle complexity at a level that was previously impossible, allowing organizations to optimize their schedules in real time, even in the face of uncertainty and change.

4. The promise of artificial intelligence and machine learning

AI and machine learning have brought transformative capabilities to the field of scheduling. Unlike traditional rule-based systems, AI-powered scheduling solutions can learn from data, recognize patterns, and make predictions. This allows them to automatically adjust schedules based on real-time information, such as changes in demand, resource availability, or external conditions.

For example, in the transportation industry, AI algorithms can be used to optimize delivery routes and schedules by analyzing traffic patterns, weather forecasts, and vehicle availability. In health care, machine learning can help hospitals optimize staff schedules by predicting patient volumes and resource needs. These AI systems can continuously improve over time as they are exposed to more data, becoming increasingly accurate and efficient [6].

Another advantage of AI-based scheduling systems is their ability to handle uncertainty. Real-world environments are often unpredictable, and traditional scheduling tools struggle to adapt to unexpected changes. AI systems, however, can incorporate uncertainty into their models, allowing them to make more robust decisions and adapt quickly when disruptions occur.

5. Optimization algorithms: The backbone of complex scheduling

Optimization algorithms are another key component of modern scheduling systems. These algorithms work by searching for the best possible solution to a scheduling problem within a set of constraints. They can evaluate millions of potential scheduling combinations in a fraction of the time it would take a human to do the same, making them ideal for handling large-scale, complex problems [7].

One of the most commonly used optimization techniques in scheduling is the *genetic algorithm*, which is inspired by the process of natural selection. This algorithm generates multiple potential solutions (or "schedules") and then selects the best ones based on predefined criteria, such as minimizing time or maximizing resource utilization. Over successive iterations, the algorithm refines these solutions, ultimately arriving at an optimal or near-optimal schedule.

Other popular optimization techniques include *linear programming*, *dynamic programming*, and *constraint satisfaction algorithms*. Each of these methods has its own strengths and weaknesses, depending on the specific nature of the scheduling problem at hand. Throughout this book, we will explore these techniques in detail, offering guidance on when and how to apply them in different contexts.

6. Bringing it all together

The objective of *Mastering Time* is to demystify the complexities of scheduling and provide readers with the knowledge and tools to apply innovative scheduling techniques in both professional and personal settings. Whether you are managing a large industrial project or simply trying to make the most of your day, the principles and solutions outlined in this book can help you achieve your goals with greater efficiency and less stress [8].

This book is divided into several sections, each focusing on different aspects of scheduling and time management. In the early chapters, we explore the nature of scheduling problems and examine why they are so challenging to solve. This includes an in-depth look at the various constraints and factors that influence scheduling decisions, such as resource availability, task dependencies, and time-sensitive priorities.

Later chapters introduce cutting-edge scheduling techniques, from AI-powered tools to advanced optimization algorithms. We will delve into how these innovations are being used across a range of industries—manufacturing, health care, logistics, and more—to revolutionize the way organizations approach time management and resource allocation. Practical case studies are included throughout to illustrate these concepts in action, showing how companies and individuals have successfully implemented innovative scheduling solutions.

The final section of the book is dedicated to personal scheduling and time management. While much of the focus is on large-scale industrial applications, the principles of effective scheduling apply equally to individual lives. We will explore how the same tools and techniques can help people better manage their time, reduce stress, and achieve a healthier work–life balance [9].

7. A path forward

Time management and scheduling will always be challenging, but with the right tools and knowledge, they can also become sources of tremendous opportunity. *Mastering Time* is about more than just solving scheduling problems—it is about changing the way we think about time, efficiency, and resource management in a world where every second counts [10].

As you work through the book, you will discover not only practical solutions to your scheduling challenges but also a new perspective on time itself. With the right mindset and techniques, even the most complex scheduling problems can be transformed into manageable, solvable puzzles—allowing you to reclaim control over your time and achieve your objectives more effectively than ever before.

Let us dive in and explore the future of scheduling together.

Author details

Ali Soofastaei
Innovative AI, Brisbane, Australia

*Address all correspondence to: ali@soofastaei.net

References

[1] Pinedo ML, Pinedo ML. Design and implementation of scheduling systems: More advanced concepts. In: Scheduling: Theory, Algorithms, and Systems. Cham, UK: Springer; 2016. pp. 485-508

[2] Gary MR, Johnson DS. Computers and Intractability: A Guide to the Theory of NP-Completeness. New York: WH Freeman and Company; 1979

[3] Baker KR, Trietsch D. Principles of Sequencing and Scheduling. USA: John Wiley and Sons; 2018

[4] Cordeau J-F et al. Transportation on demand. In: Handbooks in Operations Research and Management Science. Vol. 14. USA: Elsevier; 2007. pp. 429-466

[5] Cunha B et al. Deep reinforcement learning as a job shop scheduling solver: A literature review. In: Hybrid Intelligent Systems: 18th International Conference on Hybrid Intelligent Systems (HIS 2018). Porto, Portugal: Springer; 2020

[6] Bertsimas D, Tsitsiklis JN. Introduction to Linear Optimization. Vol. 6. Belmont, MA: Athena Scientific; 1997

[7] Lawler EL. The Traveling Salesman Problem: A Guided Tour of Combinatorial Optimization. New York, USA: Wiley-Interscience Series in Discrete Mathematics; 1985

[8] Russell SJ, Norvig P. Artificial intelligence: A modern approach. Sydney, Australia: Pearson; 2016

[9] Kolisch R, Hartmann S. Heuristic Algorithms for the Resource-Constrained Project Scheduling Problem: Classification and Computational Analysis. London, UK: Springer; 1999

[10] Laporte G, Louveaux FV. The integer L-shaped method for stochastic integer programs with complete recourse. Operations Research Letters. 1993;**13**(3):133-142

Chapter 2

Intelligent Scheduling: How AI and Advanced Analytics Are Revolutionizing Time Optimization

Ali Soofastaei

Abstract

Scheduling is critical in optimizing time and resources across industries, yet traditional scheduling methods struggle to manage the complexity and dynamic nature of modern operational environments. This chapter explores how artificial intelligence (AI) and advanced analytics transform scheduling by providing innovative solutions to age-old challenges. Through machine learning, predictive analytics, and optimization algorithms, AI-driven systems are enabling real-time decision-making and demonstrating adaptability by adjusting schedules to evolving conditions, thereby delivering higher efficiency. The chapter delves into key AI techniques such as genetic algorithms, dynamic scheduling, and multi-objective optimization, showcasing how these tools are applied in manufacturing and logistics industries. Real-world examples illustrate the tangible benefits AI offers, from reducing production downtime to improving patient care and optimizing delivery routes. This emphasis on practical value is intended to convince the audience of AI's significant impact on scheduling. Looking forward, the chapter explores emerging trends such as autonomous scheduling, the integration of AI with the Internet of Things (IoT), and the potential of quantum computing to revolutionize scheduling further. Ultimately, this chapter demonstrates that AI and advanced analytics are solving today's complex scheduling problems and reshaping the future of time optimization across industries.

Keywords: artificial intelligence (AI), advanced analytics, predictive scheduling, optimization algorithms, machine learning, genetic algorithms, dynamic scheduling, multi-objective optimization, autonomous scheduling, Internet of Things (IoT)

1. Introduction

Time optimization has long been critical for businesses, industries, and individuals. In an era where efficiency, cost control, and timely delivery are paramount, scheduling lies at the heart of nearly every operation. Whether we are looking at production lines in manufacturing, logistics and transportation, healthcare systems, or even personal time management, the complexity of scheduling has become a significant bottleneck in achieving peak performance [1].

At its core, scheduling refers to assigning resources to activities over time while adhering to various constraints. These constraints may involve deadlines, resource limitations, task dependencies, or time windows. The complexity of scheduling increases with the number of variables and constraints, and manually managing schedules is impractical for many [2].

Traditional approaches to scheduling—those based on heuristic methods, spreadsheets, or basic project management tools—are no longer adequate for today's dynamic environments. In contrast, artificial intelligence (AI) and advanced analytics have introduced a paradigm shift in addressing scheduling challenges. AI systems can learn from data, make real-time adjustments, and deliver more efficient, flexible schedules through predictive analytics, machine learning, and optimization algorithms [3].

This chapter will explore how AI and advanced analytics revolutionize scheduling, enabling organizations to optimize time and resources effectively. By leveraging the power of AI, businesses and individuals alike are making better decisions, achieving higher levels of productivity, and transforming how they manage time. The chapter will dive into specific AI techniques, real-world applications, and the potential impact of these technologies on the future of scheduling [4].

2. The role of AI in scheduling

2.1 AI and machine learning: An overview

Artificial intelligence, mainly through machine learning, has brought tremendous advancements in decision-making processes. At its core, AI refers to the ability of machines to simulate human intelligence—learning from data, recognizing patterns, and making decisions. When applied to scheduling, AI systems can do much more than automate repetitive tasks; they can intelligently adapt to changing conditions, forecast potential disruptions, and recommend optimal solutions [5].

Machine learning, a subset of AI, allows systems to learn from past data and improve over time. Machine learning algorithms analyze historical performance data in scheduling to uncover trends and patterns humans might overlook. These patterns are then used to predict future scheduling needs and prevent conflicts before they arise.

For instance, AI can analyze how long a specific task typically takes, identify recurring delays, and suggest adjustments to future schedules based on this knowledge. AI-driven systems are also capable of factoring in multiple variables, such as resource availability, time constraints, and even external factors like weather conditions, of producing optimal schedules in real time [6].

2.2 Predictive analytics in scheduling

Predictive analytics plays a vital role in scheduling by leveraging historical data to forecast future outcomes. AI systems with predictive models can anticipate potential bottlenecks, predict resource shortages, or identify tasks likely to overrun their time estimates. This capability allows organizations to be proactive rather than reactive, enabling them to make informed scheduling decisions well in advance [7].

For example, in the supply chain and logistics industry, predictive analytics is used to forecast delivery times based on factors such as traffic patterns, weather conditions, and historical data on delivery delays. AI systems analyze this data and predict when a delivery might be delayed, allowing logistics companies to adjust their schedules or notify customers in advance. These predictive models can significantly enhance efficiency by reducing idle times, minimizing resource wastage, and improving overall reliability.

Moreover, predictive scheduling models are invaluable in industries like healthcare, where patient volumes fluctuate daily. AI systems can predict peak times for patient inflow based on historical data, weather changes, and local events, allowing hospitals to adjust staff schedules to meet demand, thereby optimizing patient care and minimizing wait times [8].

2.3 AI-powered decision-making

One of the most significant contributions of AI to scheduling is its ability to support decision-making processes. Unlike traditional methods, where scheduling decisions are typically made based on fixed rules or manual adjustments, AI-driven systems use data-driven insights to recommend the most efficient scheduling options. AI algorithms can simulate thousands of potential scheduling scenarios and evaluate them based on key performance metrics such as time, cost, and resource utilization.

For example, AI-powered scheduling systems in the manufacturing industry analyze production data to automatically adjust machine operating times, shift work schedules, and optimize maintenance periods. By using real-time data from machines and production lines, these systems can make dynamic scheduling decisions to avoid bottlenecks, reduce downtime, and ensure smooth production flows [9].

In the healthcare industry, AI-powered scheduling tools help hospitals optimize staff and patient scheduling by analyzing a variety of factors, such as staff availability, patient urgency, and resource constraints. AI systems can automatically allocate staff to departments with the highest demand, ensuring that patient care is not compromised while maximizing resource utilization [10].

The key advantage of AI-powered decision-making is its ability to respond to changes in real time. In dynamic environments, such as transportation or project management, schedules are often disrupted by unforeseen events like equipment failure, employee absences, or delays in supply chains. AI systems can react to these disruptions immediately by re-optimizing schedules, reallocating resources, or recommending alternative solutions—minimizing downtime and ensuring smooth operations.

3. Advanced analytics for enhanced scheduling

3.1 Introduction to advanced analytics

Advanced analytics involves the use of sophisticated data analysis techniques to draw insights from large datasets. In scheduling, advanced analytics goes beyond simply generating schedules—it analyzes the underlying data to identify trends, uncover inefficiencies, and provide actionable recommendations for improvement. By combining statistical modeling, predictive analytics, and data mining, advanced analytics equips organizations with the tools they need to optimize schedules and enhance performance [11].

Advanced analytics can be broken down into several key types: descriptive analytics, predictive analytics, and prescriptive analytics. Each plays a vital role in addressing different aspects of scheduling challenges.

3.2 Descriptive analytics

Descriptive analytics involves analyzing historical data to understand what has happened in the past. In the context of scheduling, descriptive analytics allows organizations to gain insights into how their resources were used, where bottlenecks occurred, and which tasks or processes took longer than expected. By studying these patterns, decision-makers can identify inefficiencies and areas for improvement.

For example, a manufacturing plant might use descriptive analytics to analyze the average time taken by different machines to complete specific tasks. If certain machines consistently experience delays, it may indicate a need for maintenance, additional resources, or process adjustments. By uncovering these insights, managers can make informed decisions to improve future schedules [12].

Descriptive analytics also allows organizations to benchmark their performance. By comparing current scheduling outcomes with the past performance, decision-makers can assess whether their scheduling strategies are improving over time or if new inefficiencies have emerged.

3.3 Prescriptive analytics

Prescriptive analytics is the next step in advanced analytics, providing recommendations on the best course of action. While predictive analytics tells you what is likely to happen, prescriptive analytics goes further by suggesting what you should do in response. In scheduling, prescriptive analytics helps organizations make informed decisions by analyzing multiple possible scenarios and recommending the optimal schedule [13].

In project management, for example, prescriptive analytics can help managers determine the best way to allocate resources across tasks, ensuring that deadlines are met while minimizing costs. By simulating different resource allocation strategies, the AI-driven system can recommend the schedule that achieves the best balance between resource utilization, cost, and project timelines.

Similarly, in airline scheduling, prescriptive analytics can optimize crew schedules by considering multiple factors such as crew availability, flight durations, and time zone changes. By automatically generating optimized schedules, airlines can reduce crew fatigue, avoid scheduling conflicts, and improve operational efficiency [14].

3.4 The role of big data

In recent years, big data has become a cornerstone of advanced analytics, providing organizations with the ability to process and analyze massive datasets. Big data enables AI-driven scheduling systems to take into account a wide array of variables, including external factors such as weather conditions, traffic patterns, or economic trends, alongside internal operational data.

For instance, in supply chain and logistics, big data analytics allows companies to gather and analyze data from sensors, GPS devices, and historical delivery records to optimize routing schedules in real time. By incorporating real-time data from thousands of sources, big data analytics ensures that scheduling systems can react to changing conditions instantly, minimizing delays and optimizing resource allocation [15].

4. Optimization algorithms in scheduling

4.1 Introduction to optimization

At the heart of many advanced AI-driven scheduling systems lies the field of optimization. Optimization algorithms are designed to find the most efficient solution to a problem within a set of constraints. When it comes to scheduling, these algorithms evaluate various possible schedules and select the one that best satisfies a defined objective, whether it is minimizing time, reducing costs, or maximizing resource utilization [16].

Optimization algorithms have evolved significantly over time, and their application to scheduling has provided substantial benefits across industries. In complex environments—such as manufacturing plants, transportation networks, and even healthcare systems—optimization is essential to balancing competing priorities and resolving conflicts in scheduling.

4.2 Genetic algorithms

One of the most widely used optimization techniques in scheduling is the *genetic algorithm (GA)*. Inspired by the process of natural selection, genetic algorithms are powerful tools for solving complex scheduling problems. They work by generating a pool of potential solutions (or schedules), evaluating their fitness based on predefined criteria (such as time, cost, or resource usage), and then iteratively refining them to produce better solutions [16].

In scheduling, genetic algorithms can be especially effective when dealing with multiple constraints, such as task dependencies, limited resources, and variable durations. By simulating the process of natural evolution—through selection, crossover, and mutation—these algorithms evolve toward the optimal schedule over time.

For example, in a manufacturing environment, a genetic algorithm can optimize machine schedules by evaluating millions of potential sequences of tasks, taking into account machine availability, task durations, and maintenance requirements. The algorithm iterates over generations, refining the schedule to minimize downtime and maximize throughput [17].

Genetic algorithms are particularly useful in scheduling scenarios where there is no single "correct" solution but rather a set of competing objectives. For instance, balancing cost reduction with timely task completion often requires trade-offs. Genetic algorithms excel at identifying these trade-offs and finding schedules that strike the right balance between competing goals.

4.3 Dynamic scheduling algorithms

Traditional scheduling methods often assume a static environment, where all variables are known in advance. However, real-world scheduling problems are far more dynamic. Unforeseen events such as machine breakdowns, changes in demand, or staff unavailability can render static schedules obsolete. This is where dynamic scheduling algorithms come into play.

Dynamic scheduling algorithms are designed to adapt schedules in real time as new information becomes available. They continuously monitor the system, detect changes, and adjust the schedule accordingly to minimize disruptions. These algorithms are invaluable in industries where schedules are frequently disrupted by unexpected events [18].

For example, in the logistics industry, dynamic scheduling algorithms can re-optimize delivery routes in response to real-time traffic data or sudden changes in delivery orders. If a driver encounters heavy traffic or road closures, the dynamic scheduling system can quickly reroute the driver and adjust delivery times to ensure minimal delay.

Similarly, in manufacturing, if a machine unexpectedly goes offline for maintenance, dynamic scheduling algorithms can adjust the production schedule by reallocating tasks to other machines or rescheduling tasks in the most efficient order. This ability to respond to real-time changes enables businesses to maintain high levels of productivity, even in unpredictable environments.

4.4 Multi-objective optimization

Many scheduling problems are characterized by the need to balance multiple, often conflicting, objectives. For example, a hospital may need to optimize its staff schedules to minimize both labor costs and patient wait times while also ensuring that staffs do not exceed their working hours. Multi-objective optimization algorithms are designed to handle these types of challenges, where multiple goals need to be achieved simultaneously [19].

In multi-objective optimization, the goal is not to find a single "best" solution but rather to identify a set of solutions that offer different trade-offs between objectives. This set of solutions is often referred to as the Pareto front, where each solution represents a different balance between competing objectives. Decision-makers can then choose the solution that best aligns with their priorities.

For example, in the aviation industry, airline scheduling involves balancing factors such as crew availability, flight schedules, maintenance windows, and fuel efficiency. A multi-objective optimization algorithm can evaluate these competing goals and generate a set of possible schedules, each representing a different balance between minimizing costs and maximizing efficiency. Airline managers can then select the schedule that best meets their operational and financial requirements.

5. AI and analytics in action: Real-world applications

AI and advanced analytics have been successfully deployed across various industries, transforming the way scheduling challenges are addressed. In this section, we will explore several real-world applications that showcase the power of AI-driven scheduling solutions [20].

5.1 Manufacturing industry

In the manufacturing sector, AI-powered scheduling systems are revolutionizing the way production lines are managed. These systems optimize machine utilization, minimize downtime, and ensure that production schedules are aligned with demand.

One prominent example is the use of AI in smart factories, where machines are equipped with sensors that provide real-time data on their status. AI systems continuously monitor this data, adjusting production schedules to account for machine downtime, maintenance needs, and changes in production demand. By dynamically optimizing the production schedule, AI reduces inefficiencies and increases output [21].

Case study: A major automotive manufacturer implemented an AI-driven scheduling system to optimize its production line. The system used machine learning to analyze historical production data and predict when machines would require maintenance. By integrating predictive maintenance data into the production schedule, the manufacturer was able to reduce downtime by 20% and increase overall production efficiency.

5.2 Healthcare sector

In the healthcare sector, efficient scheduling is crucial for optimizing patient care and resource utilization. AI-driven scheduling systems are helping hospitals manage the complex tasks of allocating staff, scheduling surgeries, and managing patient appointments.

AI systems in healthcare use predictive analytics to forecast patient inflow and adjust staff schedules accordingly. For example, during flu season, AI systems can predict an increase in patient volume and recommend adjustments to staffing levels to ensure that hospitals are adequately prepared. These systems also optimize operating room schedules, minimizing downtime between surgeries and ensuring that resources such as surgical teams and equipment are used efficiently [22].

Case study: A hospital in the United States implemented an AI-based scheduling system to optimize its operating room schedules. The system analyzed historical surgery data, patient arrival patterns, and staff availability to recommend the most efficient surgery schedules. As a result, the hospital reduced patient wait times by 15% and increased the number of surgeries performed by 10%.

5.3 Supply chain and logistics

Supply chain and logistics are industries where scheduling plays a critical role in ensuring timely deliveries and minimizing operational costs. AI and advanced analytics are transforming how logistics companies optimize routes, manage fleets, and adjust schedules in real time.

In logistics, AI-powered systems use real-time data from GPS devices, traffic sensors, and weather forecasts to adjust delivery schedules and routes. These systems can dynamically re-optimize routes if traffic conditions change or if new delivery orders are added. This flexibility allows logistics companies to minimize delivery times, reduce fuel consumption, and improve overall customer satisfaction [23].

Case study: A global logistics company implemented an AI-driven scheduling system to optimize its delivery routes. The system used real-time traffic data and historical delivery performance to predict delays and recommend alternative routes. By dynamically adjusting delivery schedules, the company reduced delivery times by 12% and lowered fuel costs by 8%.

5.4 Project management

Project management involves coordinating multiple tasks and resources to meet deadlines and stay within budget. AI and advanced analytics are helping project managers optimize task sequencing, resource allocation, and risk management.

AI systems in project management use predictive analytics to identify potential delays and recommend adjustments to the project schedule. For example, if a critical task is falling behind, the AI system can recommend reallocating resources or adjusting task dependencies to keep the project on track. AI can also analyze historical project data to identify patterns of delay and suggest proactive measures to avoid similar issues in future projects [24].

Example: A construction company implemented an AI-based project management system to optimize its task schedules. The system used machine learning algorithms to predict potential delays in construction tasks based on weather data, equipment availability, and crew performance. By providing real-time recommendations, the system helped the company reduce project delays by 18%.

6. Challenges and limitations of AI and advanced analytics in scheduling

While AI and advanced analytics offer immense potential for improving scheduling efficiency, there are several challenges and limitations that organizations must consider when implementing these systems.

6.1 Data quality and availability

AI-driven scheduling systems rely heavily on data to make accurate predictions and recommendations. However, the effectiveness of these systems is directly linked to the quality and availability of the data they analyze. Inaccurate, incomplete, or outdated data can lead to suboptimal scheduling decisions, resulting in inefficiencies and delays.

Organizations must ensure that their data is accurate, up-to-date, and comprehensive. This often involves integrating data from multiple sources, such as sensors, historical records, and real-time systems. Without a solid foundation of reliable data, even the most sophisticated AI systems will struggle to deliver meaningful improvements in scheduling.

6.2 Ethical considerations

As AI systems become more integrated into scheduling, ethical considerations must be addressed. One of the most significant concerns is the potential for AI to inadvertently perpetuate bias in scheduling decisions. For instance, AI systems trained on historical data might replicate biases present in that data, such as unfair labor practices or resource allocation patterns that favor certain groups over others.

In industries like healthcare or education, biased scheduling could lead to unequal access to critical services. AI systems must be carefully designed and monitored to ensure fairness in scheduling decisions, especially in sectors where resource allocation affects people's well-being. Additionally, transparency in AI decision-making is essential, as stakeholders need to understand how and why certain scheduling recommendations are made.

Organizations should also consider the ethical implications of replacing human decision-making with AI in scheduling. While AI can optimize efficiency, it may also remove the human judgment needed to account for unique circumstances or individual needs. Striking a balance between AI-driven efficiency and human oversight is crucial for ethical scheduling practices.

6.3 System complexity

The integration of AI and advanced analytics into scheduling systems introduces a level of complexity that can be challenging for organizations to manage. Implementing AI-powered scheduling requires significant infrastructure, including data collection systems, machine learning models, and computational resources. For businesses with limited technical expertise, deploying and maintaining these systems may be a steep learning curve.

Furthermore, AI-driven scheduling solutions must be designed to integrate with existing business processes and legacy systems. Without proper integration, scheduling systems may face technical issues, such as data silos or compatibility problems with other business tools, leading to disruptions instead of improvements.

Scalability is another challenge. AI systems that work well in small-scale operations may struggle when applied to large, complex environments, particularly in industries where scheduling decisions span multiple regions, time zones, or departments. Ensuring that AI solutions are flexible and scalable is a key to maximizing their potential.

6.4 Dependence on human intervention

Despite the advanced capabilities of AI in scheduling, human intervention remains necessary. AI systems excel at processing vast amounts of data and optimizing scheduling decisions, but they cannot account for every possible nuance. There are instances where human judgment is required to adapt schedules to unforeseen circumstances, unique customer needs, or ethical concerns that an AI system may overlook.

For example, in a hospital setting, an AI system might recommend an optimal surgery schedule based on data, but a surgeon may need to adjust the schedule based on a patient's unique medical history or urgency of care. Similarly, in project management, a manager might choose to prioritize one task over another based on human intuition or stakeholder priorities, even if the AI system suggests a different sequence.

Therefore, while AI-driven systems can drastically reduce manual scheduling efforts and improve overall efficiency, a hybrid approach that combines AI with human oversight ensures that decisions are both data-driven and contextually sound.

7. Future trends in AI-driven scheduling

As AI and advanced analytics continue to evolve, the future of scheduling will be shaped by new technologies and innovations. This section explores the emerging trends that will define the next generation of AI-driven scheduling systems.

7.1 AI-enabled autonomous scheduling systems

One of the most exciting developments in the field of scheduling is the rise of fully autonomous scheduling systems. These systems aim to eliminate the need for manual intervention entirely by leveraging AI to create, adjust, and optimize schedules in real time without human input.

Autonomous scheduling systems are being explored in industries such as manufacturing, where production lines are increasingly automated. In these environments, machines communicate with each other and with AI systems to determine the most efficient production schedules based on real-time data. These systems are also being used in logistics, where autonomous fleets of vehicles and drones can be scheduled and routed by AI systems to optimize delivery times and reduce costs.

While fully autonomous scheduling is still in its early stages, the potential for these systems to revolutionize time optimization across industries is immense. In the future, we may see entire supply chains, production lines, and service industries operating with minimal human intervention driven by autonomous AI scheduling systems.

7.2 AI and IoT (Internet of Things)

The Internet of Things (IoT) refers to a network of interconnected devices that collect and exchange data. When combined with AI, IoT provides an unprecedented level of real-time data that can be used to optimize scheduling decisions. IoT devices, such as sensors, GPS trackers, and smart machines, collect data on everything from machine performance to environmental conditions, feeding this data into AI-driven scheduling systems.

For example, in smart factories, IoT devices can monitor machine health and production output in real time. If a machine shows signs of wear, an IoT sensor alerts the AI system, which then adjusts the production schedule to account for maintenance or reallocate tasks to other machines. Similarly, in the logistics industry, IoT sensors in delivery trucks provide real-time location data, enabling AI systems to dynamically adjust delivery schedules and routes based on traffic or road conditions.

As IoT technology becomes more widespread, its integration with AI will lead to more accurate, responsive, and efficient scheduling systems, particularly in industries that rely on real-time data to manage operations.

7.3 The role of generative AI in scheduling

Generative AI, which refers to AI systems capable of creating new content or solutions based on input data, is another emerging technology with significant implications for scheduling. Unlike traditional AI systems that rely on predefined rules or historical data, generative AI can create entirely new schedules based on a range of inputs and constraints.

For example, in the entertainment industry, generative AI can create personalized production schedules for film shoots, considering factors such as actor availability, weather conditions, and location logistics. Similarly, in healthcare, generative AI can be used to create custom treatment schedules for patients based on their medical history and current health status.

The flexibility of generative AI allows it to explore creative solutions to scheduling problems that may not have been considered by traditional methods. As this technology advances, we may see more organizations adopting generative AI to tackle complex, multi-variable scheduling challenges in innovative ways.

7.4 AI and quantum computing

Quantum computing, still in its infancy, holds enormous potential for transforming AI-driven scheduling. Traditional computing systems process information in binary (0s and 1s), but quantum computers operate using quantum bits (qubits), which can represent multiple states simultaneously. This capability allows quantum computers to process vast amounts of data exponentially faster than classical computers.

For scheduling, quantum computing could revolutionize optimization algorithms by enabling the rapid evaluation of millions of possible scheduling scenarios in real time. Industries that require extremely complex scheduling, such as pharmaceuticals, aerospace, or large-scale infrastructure projects, stand to benefit significantly from quantum computing's ability to solve optimization problems that are currently too complex for even the most advanced AI systems.

Although quantum computing is not yet widely available, research is ongoing, and early applications in scheduling are expected to emerge within the next decade. When quantum computing becomes more accessible, it will likely redefine the boundaries of what is possible in AI-driven scheduling systems.

8. Enhanced methodologies, case studies, and comparative analysis

8.1 Methodologies in intelligent scheduling

AI-driven scheduling methodologies are built on a foundation of advanced algorithms and analytics. This section elaborates on the core methodologies, complemented by visual schematics for clarity.

1. *Genetic algorithms*: These simulate evolutionary processes to optimize schedules. The algorithm iteratively improves upon a pool of candidate solutions.

2. *Dynamic scheduling*: This technology adapts schedules in real time to changing conditions, leveraging sensor inputs and IoT data streams.

3. *Multi-objective optimization*: Balances conflicting objectives using Pareto optimality, such as cost minimization and efficiency maximization (**Figure 1**).

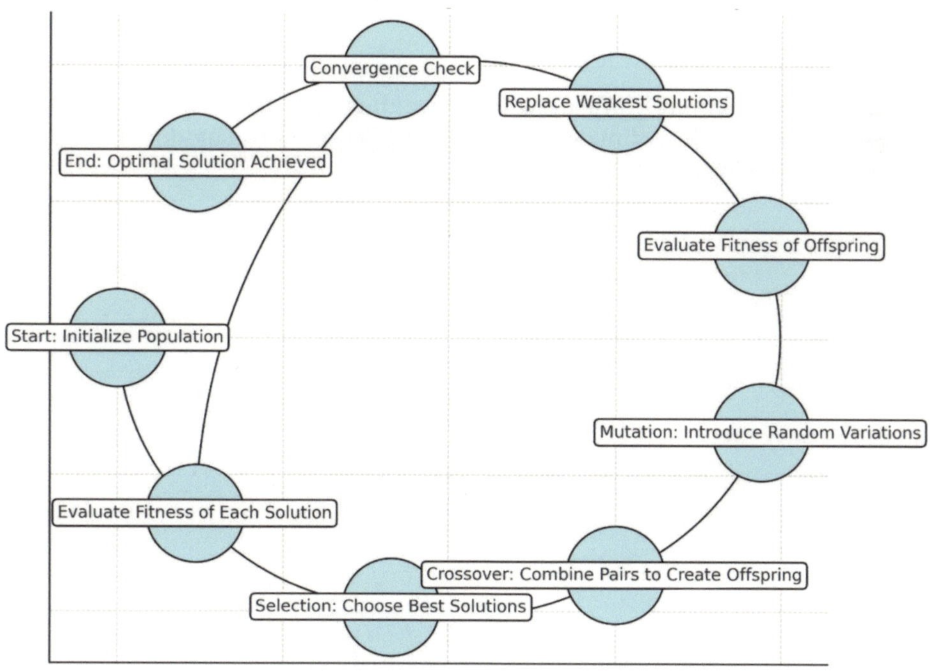

Figure 1.
Flowchart of genetic algorithm for scheduling.

8.2 Supplementary materials

To support readers in applying these methodologies, supplementary resources are provided:

- *Sample datasets*: Historical scheduling data for manufacturing, logistics, and healthcare industries.
- *Software tools*: Links to open-source platforms like Python libraries (Scikit-learn, TensorFlow) and visualization tools (Tableau, Matplotlib).
- *Demonstrative code snippets*: Python code implementing a basic genetic algorithm for scheduling (**Table 1**).

Metric	Traditional scheduling	AI-driven scheduling
Efficiency	Manual, time-consuming	Automated, real time
Adaptability	Limited	High, react to disruptions
Resource utilization	Suboptimal	Optimized using algorithms
Predictive insights	None	Advanced predictive models

Table 1.
Comparative analysis: AI-driven vs. traditional scheduling.

9. Case studies

9.1 Manufacturing sector

Scenario: Implementation of a dynamic scheduling system in a smart factory.
Numerical impact: Downtime was reduced by 20%, and production efficiency increased by 25% (**Figure 2**).

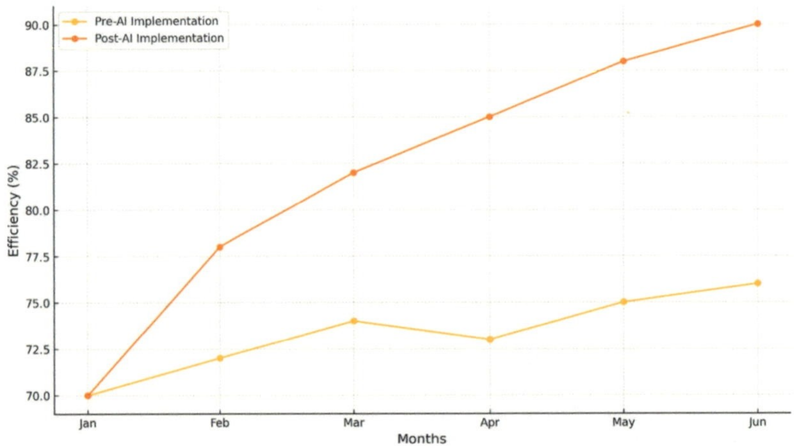

Figure 2.
Line graph illustrating production efficiency over 6 months pre- and post-AI implementation.

9.2 Healthcare sector

Scenario: Optimizing staff and patient scheduling in a metropolitan hospital.

Numerical impact: Patient wait times decreased by 15%, and staff utilization improved by 30% (**Table 2**).

Metric	Before AI	After AI
Downtime (%)	15	8
Production efficiency (%)	75	90
Operational cost reduction (%)	5	20

Table 2.
Breakdown of operational metrics before and after AI adoption.

9.3 Logistics and supply chain

Scenario: Route optimization using predictive analytics for a delivery company.

Numerical impact: Delivery times were reduced by 12%, and fuel consumption was lowered by 8% (**Figure 3**).

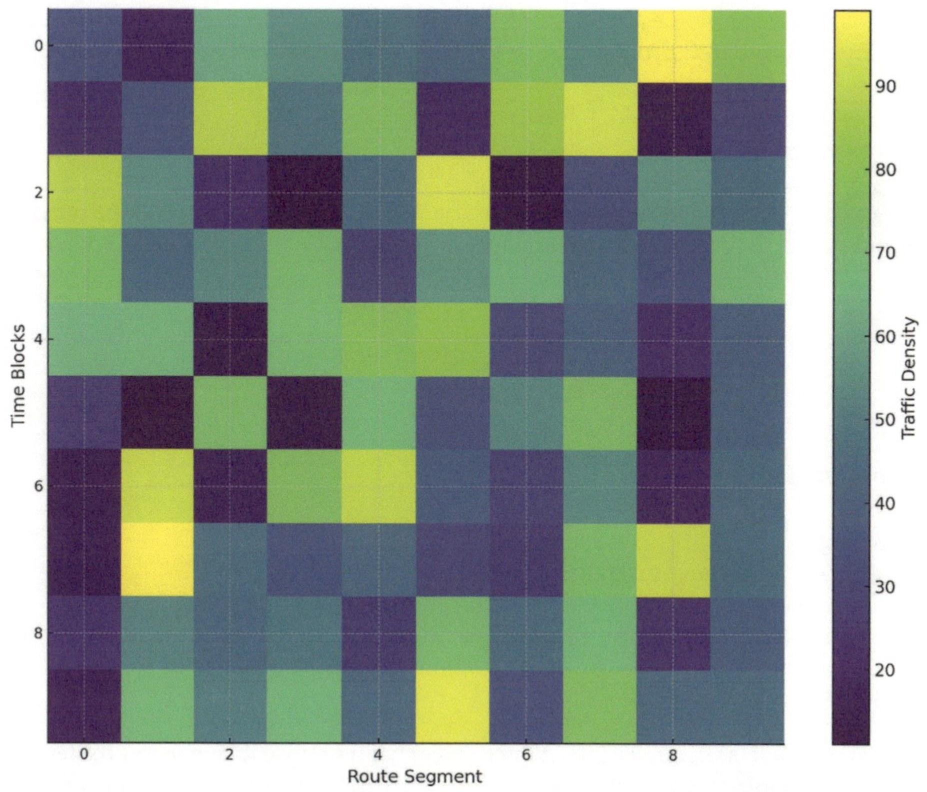

Figure 3.
Heatmap showing traffic patterns and optimized delivery routes.

10. Conclusion

Integrating AI and advanced analytics into scheduling transforms industries and revolutionizes how organizations manage their time and resources. From predictive analytics that anticipate scheduling conflicts to optimization algorithms that streamline resource allocation, AI-driven systems provide businesses with powerful tools to overcome the complexities of modern scheduling.

Throughout this chapter, we have explored the multifaceted role of AI in scheduling, from machine learning models that enhance decision-making to advanced optimization algorithms that tackle multi-variable scheduling challenges. We have also seen real-world examples of how AI and analytics improve efficiency in sectors as diverse as manufacturing, healthcare, logistics, and project management.

While challenges remain—such as data quality, system complexity, and ethical considerations—the potential benefits of AI-driven scheduling are undeniable. As technology advances, we expect to see even more sophisticated scheduling systems combining AI with emerging innovations like IoT, generative AI, and quantum computing.

The future of scheduling lies in intelligent systems that optimize time and adapt to dynamic environments, making real-time decisions with minimal human intervention. In this new era of AI-driven scheduling, organizations will be empowered to unlock unprecedented productivity, efficiency, and innovation levels.

Ultimately, mastering time through intelligent scheduling is not just about improving business processes—it is about rethinking how we approach time. With the right tools and technologies, scheduling can evolve from a complex challenge into a streamlined, automated process that drives industry success.

Acknowledgements

The author acknowledges the use of artificial intelligence to enhance the writing style and polish the manuscript's language.

Author details

Ali Soofastaei
Innovative AI, Brisbane, Australia

*Address all correspondence to: ali@soofastaei.net

References

[1] Pinedo ML, Pinedo ML. Design and implementation of scheduling systems: More advanced concepts. In: Scheduling: Theory, Algorithms, and Systems. New York, USA: Springer; 2016. pp. 485-508

[2] Gary MR, Johnson DS. Computers and Intractability: A Guide to the Theory of NP-Completeness. New York: WH Freeman and Company; 1979

[3] Baker KR, Trietsch D. Principles of Sequencing and Scheduling. Hoboken, New Jersey, USA: John Wiley & Sons; 2018

[4] Cordeau J-F et al. Transportation on demand. In: Handbooks in Operations Research and Management Science. Vol. 14. Amsterdam, Netherlands: Elsevier; 2007. pp. 429-466

[5] Kolasani S. Revolutionizing manufacturing, making it more efficient, flexible, and intelligent with Industry 4.0 innovations. International Journal of Sustainable Development Through AI, ML and IoT. 2024;**3**(1):1-17

[6] Bertsimas D, Tsitsiklis JN. Introduction to Linear Optimization. Vol. 6. Belmont, MA: Athena Scientific; 1997

[7] Russell SJ, Norvig P. Artificial Intelligence: A Modern Approach. Hoboken, New Jersey, USA: Pearson; 2016

[8] Kolisch R, Hartmann S. Heuristic Algorithms for the Resource-Constrained Project Scheduling Problem: Classification and Computational Analysis. Berlin, Germany: Springer; 1999

[9] Lawler EL. The Traveling Salesman Problem: A Guided Tour of Combinatorial Optimization. Wiley-Interscience Series in Discrete Mathematics. Hoboken, New Jersey, USA: Wiley-Intercedence; 1985

[10] Bertolini M et al. Machine learning for industrial applications: A comprehensive literature review. Expert Systems with Applications. 2021;**175**:114820

[11] Laporte G, Louveaux FV. The integer L-shaped method for stochastic integer programs with complete recourse. Operations Research Letters. 1993;**13**(3):133-142

[12] Barak S, Moghdani R, Maghsoudlou H. Energy-efficient multi-objective flexible manufacturing scheduling. Journal of Cleaner Production. 2021;**283**:124610

[13] Deb K. Nonlinear goal programming using multi-objective genetic algorithms. Journal of the Operational Research Society. 2001;**52**(3):291-302

[14] Bertsimas D, Stellato B. Online mixed-integer optimization in milliseconds. INFORMS Journal on Computing. 2022;**34**(4):2229-2248

[15] Holland, John H. Adaptation in Nature and Artificial Systems. Ann Arbor, Michigan, USA: The University of Michigan Press; 1975

[16] Fox MS, Smith SF. ISIS—A knowledge-based system for factory scheduling. Expert Systems. 1984;**1**(1):25-49

[17] Lee YH, Pinedo M. Scheduling jobs on parallel machines with sequence-dependent setup times. European Journal of Operational Research. 1997;**100**(3):464-474

[18] Silver EA, Pyke DF, Peterson R. Inventory Management and Production Planning and Scheduling. Vol. 3. New York: Wiley; 1998

[19] Gill SS et al. AI for next generation computing: Emerging trends and future directions. Internet of Things. 2022;**19**:100514

[20] Manimaran G, Murthy CSR. An efficient dynamic scheduling algorithm for multiprocessor real-time systems. IEEE Transactions on Parallel and Distributed Systems. 1998;**9**(3):312-319

[21] Hoffman KL, Padberg M, Rinaldi G. Traveling salesman problem. In: Encyclopedia of Operations Research and Management Science. Vol. 1. New York, USA: Springer; 2013. pp. 1573-1578

[22] Otchere DA. Data Science and Machine Learning Applications in Subsurface Engineering. Boca Raton, Florida, USA: CRC Press, Taylor & Francis Group; 2024

[23] Beasley JE. OR-library: Distributing test problems by electronic mail. Journal of the Operational Research Society. 1990;**41**(11):1069-1072

[24] Mohammadbagherpoor H, et al. Exploring airline gate-scheduling optimization using quantum computers. arXiv Preprint arXiv:2111.09472, 2021

Chapter 3

IoT Based Automatic Intravenous Bag Data Logging Monitoring and Alert System

S. Sriram, G. Rajeshkumar, K. Saranya, E. Saranya, R. Kavitha and A. Madhumitha

Abstract

Saline, one of the most widely used intravenous (IV) medications, is essential in the treatment of critically ill patients. Monitoring the fluid level in the saline bottle is crucial because blood flows return to the bottle when the fluid level is empty as still needle is present in the patient's vein. The proper timing of withdrawing the needle from the patient's vein is usually ignored due to carelessness and any unusual circumstances result in danger. In addition, health services can be focused on the issue through remote monitoring. To avoid the accident due to caregiver ignorance, we designed a cost-effective intelligent saline level for supervision in health monitoring system that combines sensor and Internet of Things (IOT) technology. This system was created using load cell with a cheap, very low power microcontroller. The load of the bottle is converted to the selected voltage through the load sensor. The ESP8266 microcontroller generates and publishes a specific message based on voltage received from the sensor and forwards them to health professionals. The proposed monitoring system delivers message to subscribers in a reliable manner, which is crucial for the healthcare industry. Then, with the help of a human, the valve of the saline bottle is closed.

Keywords: saline, Internet of Things, contactless liquid level sensor, microcontroller, medicine box

1. Introduction

Internet of things (IOT) is a network of physical objects made up of all gadgets, cars, buildings and other things that include electronics, software and sensors that allow them to interact with each other [1]. Due to the convergence of many technologies such as real-time analytics, machine learning, cheap sensors and embedded systems, IOT has advanced facilities in terms of communication. Whenever a patient is given saline, the patient is closely watched by a nurse or other family members. Mostly due to carelessness, lack of focus, busy schedule and increasing number of patients, nurses forget to replace the saline bottle fluid level at the ending stage. Due to the pressure difference between the empty saline bottle and the blood, the blood returns to the saline bottle immediately after the saline is exhausted. This allows the patient's veins to reverse blood flow to the saline vessel. This causes the patient's hemoglobin levels to drop, and can also cause a shortage of red blood cells (RBCs) in the patient's blood, leading them to feel tired. Therefore, a salt-level monitoring system must be created to somewhat reduce the patient's dependence on nurses or other caregivers. This system uses an automatic warning and signaling device based on arduino. When the intravenous fluid level falls below a specified threshold, the load cell's output voltage level changes. The nurse is notified by an alarm that the patient's saline supply has been exhausted as soon as the saline drops to a certain low level. The difference in weight is used to identify the amount of salt in the bottle and send an SMS alert. If the nurse does not approach the patient immediately, a motor is arranged that flattens and compresses the saline tube to stop functioning.

2. Related work

An electronic valve module usually includes closed solenoid valves and relays. For measurement purpose, the module uses an impeller hole flow sensor, which connects to the counter of the control module to collect and process the pulse signal of load cells for continuous monitoring The bottle weight of saline will be displayed on the LCD display. When critical level is reached, automatic message will be sent to the Android application of Hospital Staff [2, 3]. The load sensor is fixed on the saline hanger and a bottle is hung on it. This sensor calculates the bottle weight changes at different voltages. The output voltage is given from the load sensor ESP32 WIFI chip. Pressure of Drip IV solution is detected by a pressure sensor, connected to the motor control of dripping solutions is enhanced when connected to motor. Wireless transfers are made from the patient's room to nurse station effectively using the nRF24L01 module. High-performance electro-hydraulic proportional valve controller is designed and developed using embedded computers. The technology of this controller provides the simplest culture, high quality and economical and flexible operation. The flow pulse signal is collected from the valve impeller hole flow sensor through load sensor. This will sense the weight load sensor Glucose and display edit and Sends data to hospital staff's Android app.

The specially fabricated RF tag can be attached to any kind of IV liquid package available in the market. Zhang et al. developed a novel RFID-based intravenous infusion monitoring based on fork-type light barrier as a sensor using Zigbee protocol, which helps in monitoring the velocity of IV system with high accuracy and reliability. Bhavsar et al. developed intravenous fluid monitoring system where load cell checks the level of the fluid by weighing the IV bag. A drip infusion of IOT-based intravenous infusion system is suggested where it consists of various infusion monitoring devices that help in detecting the infusion rate and the collected data is send to the central monitor placed at the nurse station so that required action can be taken. Yananet a developed a health information alarm system using Bluetooth and GPRS technologies in which the system monitors, collects data and sends information to analyze counter using artificial intelligence that developed a drip monitoring system based on electrical impedance [4, 5].

The electrodes used are in non-contact with the system that determines parameters of each fluid drop. A Smart and Pervasive ICU system is developed based on Automatic Detection of Risk situation and Alert Method that consists of multi-camera system and collaborative sensor network that helps in real-time monitoring on the patients especially facing danger and chronic conditions. Rachman developed a monitoring system regarding patient infusion where laser photodiode is used. This sensor kit collects, process and further sends data to Zigbee transmission device to display them in the form of GUI. Yadav and Jain developed real-time E-saline monitoring system where IR sensor is used to detect drop rate and infusion capacity and servo meter is used to control drip rate mechanism [5, 6]. From the above literature survey, technologies such as RFID, Zigbee, GPRS are used for IV infusion monitoring. Further, IoT-based IV infusion monitoring and alerting system is very rarely seen in the literature. Keeping this in view point, IoT-based IV infusion monitoring and alerting system is designed [7].

3. Methodology

The project aims to create a smart medicine box for patients who require long-term medication and have difficulty remembering to take their pills on time. After observing these issues in hospitals and among people with these conditions, we decided to develop a smart medicine box that could address these problems. Our system utilizes push buttons to set a timetable for prescribed medications, which is stored in an RTC module. The notification times are then saved in EEPROM. When the time arrives to take medicine, the system generates a notification sound and illuminates the corresponding pill box with a bright light. This allows the patient to easily locate the correct box and take up the medicine at the prescribed time. All pill boxes are pre-loaded into the system that is able to sense whether the patient has taken their medication or not. One advantage of our system is its ability to detect whether the patient is attempting to postpone taking their medication by quickly opening and closing the pill boxes to stop the notification sound. In contrast to other devices on the market that only generate a notification sound once and then stop, our system provides ongoing reminders until the medication is taken. Overall, our system provides a fast and effective way to improve patient health by ensuring that medication is taken on time.

4. Experimental work

As per **Figure 1** block diagram of esp8266 microcontroller list below

- Pic Micro Controller
- LCD
- Limit Switch
- Contactless Liquid-Level Sensor
- Keypad
- Voice Playback Module
- LED Indicator

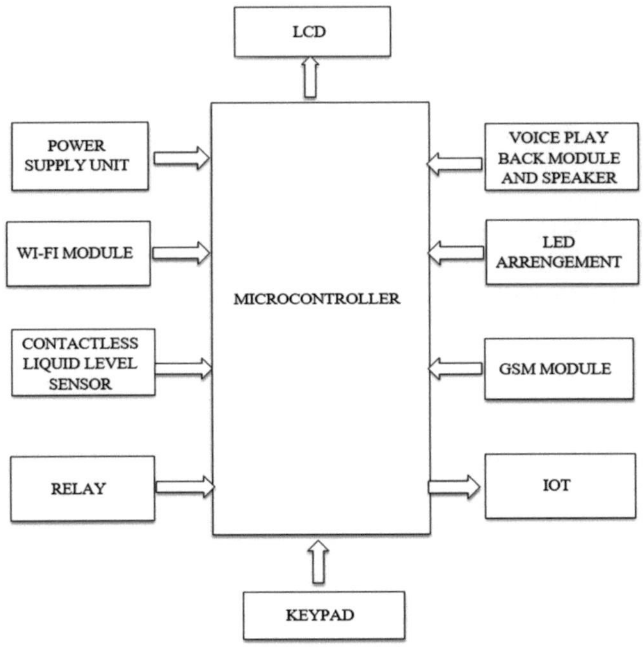

Figure 1.
Block diagram of ESP8266 microcontroller.

- GSM
- Esp8266
- Wi-Fi Module
- RTC Module

4.1 Microcontroller

A microcontroller is a small and self-contained computer that is integrated into a single chip. It is designed to handle a specific task in an embedded system and is often a low-cost solution for various applications. In simple terms, it is a programmable silicon chip that is clock-based, register-based, and capable of accepting input and providing output after processing it according to the instructions stored in its memory [8, 9].

The concept of a microcontroller involves integrating various components of a microprocessor system onto a single chip. It typically includes a CPU core, both ROM and RAM memory, and some parallel digital input/output (I/O). Additionally, microcontrollers may have the components like a timer module to do tasks for specific time periods, a serial I/O port to allow data transfer between the controller and other devices, and an ADC to process analog input data.

Compared to traditional computers, microcontrollers are smaller in size, consume less power, and are relatively inexpensive. They can perform functions on their own hardware as I/O ports and external memory [10, 11]. The CPU core is the heart of the microcontroller, and in the past, it was typically based on an 8-bit microprocessor unit such as the Motorola 6800 core found in their 6805/6808 microcontroller devices. Nowadays, microcontrollers are often designed around specifically tailored CPU cores, such as the Microchip PIC range of microcontrollers [12].

4.2 Special features of ESP8266 microcontroller

This microcontroller has a powerful RISC CPU with 35 one-word instructions, which can be executed in 1 cycle for program branches that take 2 cycles. It can operate at a clock input speed of up to 20 MHz. Other features of this microcontroller include an eight-level deep hardware stack, multiple addressing modes, power-on reset, power-up timer, oscillator start-up timer, and watchdog timer. It also has programmable code protection, a power-saving sleep mode, and low power consumption. In-circuit serial programming and debugging are available *via* two pins, and there is read/write access to processor program memory. The microcontroller can handle high source current at 25 Ma and be designed for use in commercial and industrial temperature ranges (**Figure 2**).

4.3 Peripheral features

The peripheral features of microcontroller interval between the times of the event are given in **Table 1**.

Automatic IV Bag Monitoring and Alert System monitors the IV bag data system and also monitoring the patient medicine data. The data will be automatically logged

Figure 2.
Automatic IV Bag Monitoring and Alert system.

Timer 0	8-bit counter with 8-bit prescaler
Timer1	16-bit counter with prescaler, increment able during sleep by clock
Timer2	8-bit counter with 8-bit period register, prescaler and post scaler
Capture	16-bit and maximum resolution upto 12.5 ns.
Comparison	16-bit and maximum resolution upto 200 ns.
The resolution	10-bit multi-channel analog-to-digital convert

Table 1.
Peripheral features of microcontroller intervals.

as well as stored in IOT Online Transmission. It is easy to operate and convenient for all patients, doctors and nurses. Functioning process is easier for a single individual to manage multiple patients.

5. Results and discussion

This IOT Intravenous Fluid Monitoring uses a contactless liquid-level sensor to detect as the fluid level in the IV Infusion bottle goes down and transmits the data over IOT. Once the system detects that the bottle has gone empty, it sends an alert over IOT. This chapter addresses the consequences of negligence of IV flow monitoring. Using the suggested monitoring, one can monitor the saline level from the bottle. Remote mode will help create smart health care system. An affordable, accurate and efficient system works simply. Electronic valve with a quantitative control system, to realize flow control in drops, represents small, compact and advanced technology in the medical field. A steady flow here the medicine reaches

Figure 3.
Medicine and trips in IOT.

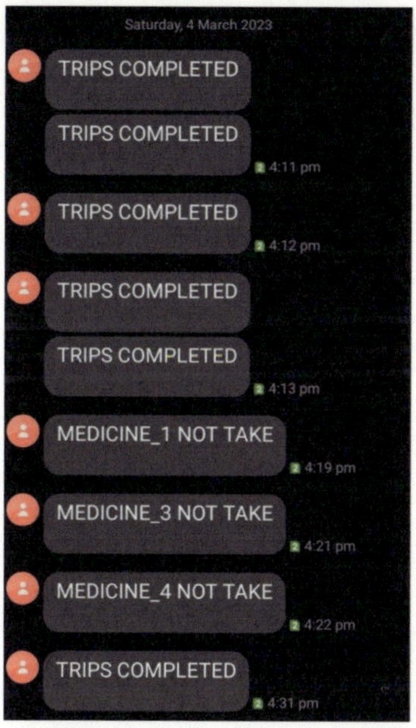

Figure 4.
SMS for not taking medicine.

the patient automatically through drops Controlled for three different flow rates 25, 50, 75% IV cannula pipe. This can be done by measuring. The level and mass of the drug through the drops is compared when it reaches the medicine point and flow stops after the desired critical point. Here, IOT replaces manual switches. Through software like user-friendly mobile apps, doctors can control the flow rate while sitting on the spot. IOT Concept Models can be implemented for remote places like villages. Doctors can sit in different cities, abuilding, or in their home and the patient may be anywhere; monitoring and flow rate control are possible. Using similar IOT concepts allows one doctor to monitor multiple patient reports on mobile app or computer screen so that a doctor can supervise many patients. Medicine and trips in IOT are shown in **Figure 3**.

SMS for not taking medicine and trips-completed message notification areis indicated in screenshot mentioned in **Figure 4**.

6. Conclusion

This study proposes an IOT-based monitoring and control platform for IV setup inspiration. Suggested work reduces the amount of time and effort. Essential for monitoring infusion setups allows for wireless monitoring. This system can be quickly installed on the stand where the drip bottle is hung, which makes a bottle replacement easier. It helps to ensure that there is zero margin of error for improper administration. Drops can lead to many problems. It also improves clinical efficacy, safety and the patient experience in hospitals and home care is possible for many patients and we additionally add medicine reminder that helps the patients.

Acknowledgements

The first version was published as a preprint, and stated under title, IOT Based Automatic Intravenous Bag Data Logging Monitoring and Alert System. *Preprint server at Research Square, posted 05 May, 2023.*

Conflict of interest

There is no conflict of interest.

Author details

S. Sriram[1*], G. Rajeshkumar[2], K. Saranya[3], E. Saranya[4], R. Kavitha[2] and A. Madhumitha[5]

1 Faculty of Associate, School of Computing, Amrita Vishwa Vidyapeetham, Amrita University, Coimbatore, Tamil Nadu, India

2 Computer Engineering Department, Bannari Amman Institute of Technology, Sathyamangalam, Tamil Nadu, India

3 Information Technology, Dr. Mahalingam College of Engineering and Technology, Pollachi, Tamil Nadu, India

4 Information Technology, Sri Eshwar College of Engineering, Coimbatore, Tamil Nadu, India

5 School of Computing, Bannari Amman Institute of Technology, Sathyamangalam, Tamil Nadu, India

*Address all correspondence to: srsriramengg1@gmail.com

References

[1] Noor F, Swaid M, Almesnad M, Almuzini N. A method for detecting the width of objects with ultrasonics sensor. In: 2018 International Conference on Computing, Electronics and Communication Engineering (iCCECE). IEEE xplore; 2018

[2] Ibrahim SN, Hakeem MSL, Asnavi AL, Malik NA. Using an automated water tank filtration system international conference on LDR sensors. In: 2016 Computer and Communication Engineering (ICCCE). IEEE xplore; 2016

[3] Sanjay B, Sanju Vikasini RM. IOT based drips surveillance in hospitals 2020. International Research Journal of Engineering and Technology (IRJET). 2020;**7**(4):1352-1353

[4] Arfan M, Srinivasan M, Baragur AG, Naveen V. Innovative, design and development of an IoT enabled IV infusion rate monitoring and control device for precision care and portability. In: 2020 4th International Conference on Electronics, Communication and Aerospace Technology (ICECA). IEEE xplore; 2020

[5] More A, Bhor D, Tilak M, Nagre G. IoT based smart saline bottle for healthcare. International Research Journal of Engineering and Technology (IRJET). 2021;**10**(6):945-946

[6] Jiang S, He Y. Low power circuit for medical drip infusion monitoring system. In: 2020 IEEE International Conference on Smart Internet of Things (Smart IoT). IEEE xplore; 2020

[7] Setiawan AW, Yenas N, Welson D. Design and realization of low-cost wireless remote infusion international seminar on monitoring system. In: 2018 Application of Information Technology and Communication. IEEE xplore; 2018

[8] Giaquinto N, Scarpetta M, Ragolia MA, Pappalardi P. By real-time drip infusion monitoring computer vision systems. In: 2020 IEEE International Symposium on Medical Measurements and Applications (MeMeA). IEEE xplore; 2020

[9] Axley B, Speranza-Reid J, Williams H. Venous needle dislodgement in patients on hemodialysis. Nephrology Nursing Journal. 2012;**39**(6):435-445

[10] Lin C-H, Chen W-L, Li C-M, et al. Assistive technology using integrated flexible sensor and virtual alarm unit for blood leakage detection during dialysis therapy. IET Healthcare Technology Letters. 2016;**3**(4):290-296. DOI: 10.1049/htl.2016.0051

[11] Brogi A, Forti S. QoS-Aware Deployment of IoT Applications through the Fog. Pisa: Technical Reports of the Department of Computing, Università di Pisa; 2016

[12] Skala K, Davidovic D, Afgan E, et al. Scalable distributed computing hierarchy: Cloud, fog, and dew computing. Open Journal of Cloud Computing. 2015;**2**:16-24

Chapter 4

An Insertion Procedure to Solve Hybrid Multiobjective Permutation Flowshop Scheduling Problems

Hafed Motair

Abstract

This paper presents an insertion procedure (IP) that can be used to improve the performance of multiobjective scheduling problems (MOSPs) algorithms. The proposed procedure uses variable neighborhood search (VNS) combined with an insertion method, which can be adapted to any MOSP, whether heuristic or metaheuristic. The aim is to solve 2-machine permutation flowshop scheduling problem (PFSP) and minimize two objective functions simultaneously: Maximum completion time (makespan) and total completion times ($\sum_j C_j$) (TCT) in order to find the efficient (non dominated) solutions. The proposed IP is combined with two algorithms from the literature, the non dominated sorting genetic algorithm (NSGA-2) and the multiobjective partial enumeration algorithm (MOPE), the objective is to explore more non dominating solution by the use of insertion concept of jobs through all possible positions of the considered sequence. To evaluate the algorithms, a large set of test instances involving up to 80 jobs was used for our investigation. We found that using the IP procedure is very useful in improving the performance of multiobjective algorithms and that the proposal was very useful in producing good solutions compared to the original algorithms, as it used to improve the performance of both MOPE and MOGA.

Keywords: multiobjective scheduling, hybrid algorithms, VNS, permutation flowshop, genetic algorithm

1. Introduction

The main objective of **job** shop problems is to find a schedule of n jobs $\{s_1, s_2, \dots, s_n\}$ that can be processed on m machines $\{W_1, W_2, \dots, W_m\}$ to optimize (minimize) a particular criterion. If the jobs pass between machines in the same order, then the resulting problem is a flowshop scheduling problem (FSP), hence the number of possible schedules are "$(n!)^m$". If we restricted the permutation of jobs for all machines is the same, then the result is a permutation flowshop scheduling problem (PFSP), and the number of possible schedules is (n!) [1].

In this work we study the 2-machine PFSP to minimize two objective functions simultaneously: makespan and total completion times, the aim is to find efficient solutions that minimize these two objective functions simultaneously, the problem denoted: $F_2||\left(C_{max}, \sum_j C_j\right)$.

In general, a MOSPs can be described as follows: Given k objective functions $\mu_1(x), \mu_2(x), \ldots, \mu_k(x)$, W is a set of feasible solutions and x is a solution, then a solution $x \in W$ is dominate a solution $y \in W$ if and only if these two conditions hold:

1. $\mu_i(x) \leq \mu_i(y), \forall i, 1 \leq i \leq k$

2. $\exists j, 1 \leq j \leq k, \mu_j(x) < \mu_j(y)$. A solution $x \in W$ is an efficient solution if there is no solution $y \in W$ dominate it.

The problem considered in this work belongs to the class of NP-hard problems in strong since [2], therefore, it may be reasonable to construct an acceptable algorithm with reasonable computational times to solve these problems even if it does not guarantee an optimal solution.

The method of finding non-dominated solutions is often expensive in terms of algorithm time and solution quality. Either the algorithm is given enough time to work and thus find acceptable solutions, in which case it will take practically unacceptable time to produce these solutions, or the time is reduced at the expense of the quality of the solutions. Therefore, we started with the idea of using the insertion method with hybridization to produce good solutions in a practical reasonable time. This method of work is not new, but we tried to add the idea to the proposal and found that it is a good addition in this field.

In this work, we improve two multi-objective PFSPs, the first one is non dominating sorting genetic algorithm (NSGA III) [3], and the second is a partial enumeration heuristic [4]. We propose the IP to improve the performance of the considered algorithms. The proposed procedure uses the VNS combined with the insertion algorithm to extend the search space of the considered algorithms to more reasonable efficient solution. Hence the proposed algorithms can be viewed as hybrid algorithms. These algorithms can be seen as complementary tools that can be imparted together to achieve an optimization goal [5].

2. Literature review

Various hybrid approaches have been proposed in the literature, these approaches are based on evolutionary algorithms, heuristics, VNS, etc. Ref. [6] combined branch and bound with genetic algorithm to minimize the two objective functions: makespan and mean flow time in the 2-machine flowshop problem. Ref. [7] used the concept of Pareto optimal solutions and proposed a multiobjective genetic algorithm to minimize the two objectives (makespan and total tardiness) and three objectives (makespan, total flow time, and total tardiness). Ref. [7] combined a local search with a genetic algorithm, the proposed a multiobjective algorithm called a hybrid genetic algorithm. Ref. [8] proposed a neighborhood search (local search) for every generation of the genetic algorithm, he used two different utility functions: a weighted linear function and a weighted Chebyshev function.to solve bi-objective functions or three objectives for multiobjective FSP. Ref. [9] proposed two hybrid multiobjective m machine no wait FSPs: hybrid simulated annealing algorithm and hybrid genetic algorithm, the objective is to minimize the weighted sum of makespan and maximum lateness criteria. Ref. [10] proposed A hybrid multiobjective genetic algorithm to solve simultaneously three objectives: makespan, mean flow time and mean tardiness times. Ref. [11] proposed a hybrid multiobjective algorithm. Various test problems are examined and metrics are evaluated in simulation, the objective is to explore Pareto optimal solutions for the given problem. Ref. [12] presents a hybrid multiobjective particle swarm optimization for multiobjective PFSPs, several adaptive local search methods were utilized to perform the test of efficiency. Ref. [13] proposed a hybrid multiobjective FSP using a local search method, the objective is to find the Pareto optimal solutions of four objective problems. Ref. [13] proposes a framework of hybrid evolutionary multiobjective optimization. For implementation of this framework, they consider the following multiobjective algorithms: NSGAII, MOEA/D, and MOEA/D. A local search is implemented and a result for simulation shows the efficiency of the proposed algorithm. Ref. [14] proposed a hybrid multiobjective genetic algorithm for FSP and a local searcher (simulated annealing is used to improve the proposed algorithm performance. An upper bound and lower bound were obtained to solve two separate single problems to validate the Pareto fronts. Ref. [15] developed a Group Decision Support System to evaluate eight flexible manufacturing systems (FMSs). Also developed an integrated approach for the decision-making problem which combines the Fuzzy Analytical Hierarchy Process (FAHP) and the Preference Ranking Organization Method for Enrichment Evaluation (PROMETHEE) method, the FAHP is used to finds weights for each criterion and the PROMETHEE used to get the final ranking. Both FAHP and PROMETHEE are in conjunction with the Geometrical Analysis for Interactive Assistance (GAIA) method to take the DMs through a series of intuitive and analytical methods. Ref. [16] proposed a hybrid artificial bee colony with adaptive neighborhood search to obtain initial processing sequence also non dominating sorting procedure was used. Finally, a simulation study was used to evaluate the proposed algorithm and the comparison made with traditional multiobjective algorithms. Ref. [17] proposed a hybrid artificial bee colony algorithm (LABC) for solving the multiobjective (flexible task) scheduling problem to optimize three objectives: makespan, maximum workload, and total workload simultaneously. A set of well-known benchmark instances was used to test the performance of the proposed algorithm, and the results showed the efficiency of the proposed algorithm. Ref. [18] addressed hybrid an energy-aware multiobjective FSP to minimize simultaneously makespan and the energy consumptions to obtain efficient solutions. They proposed two efficient crossovers: single-point Pareto crossover and two-point Pareto crossover. Ref. [19] proposed an improved SPEA2 algorithm to solve the multiobjective decision-making of investment. They used an external archive set for local search for every generation also a new crossover operator was proposed. The experimental results showed the efficiency of the improved method which can converge to the Pareto optimal solutions and improve the convergence speed. Ref. [20] proposed a multiobjective hybrid FSP, the objective is to find efficient solutions that minimize the makespan, the weighted sum of the tardiness, and the weighted sum of the earliness. Multi-objective general VNS proposed. In the simulation study, the proposed algorithm compared with four other algorithms: NSGA-II, VNS, and another MO-GVNS. The results showed the efficiency of the proposed algorithm. Ref. [21] studied the permutation flow shop scheduling problem to minimize simultaneously two objective functions, total flow time and total energy consumption. They developed a bi-objective mixed-integer programming model formulation by using a speed-scaling framework; to find the non dominated solutions of the problem, they proposed two multi-objective iterated greedy algorithms and a multiobjective variable block insertion heuristic as well as a novel construction heuristic to generate an initial solution. Experimental results showed the effectiveness of the proposed algorithms. Ref. [22] proposed a modified version of the multiobjective evolutionary algorithm based on decomposition (MOEA/D), the objective is to minimize simultaneously four cost functions; the average sojourn time, the energy consumption in the last stage, the earliness and the tardiness values. Mutation and crossover heuristics and others are developed. Computational comparisons and statistical analysis showed the effective performance of the proposed algorithms.

3. Problem constrains and formulation

The general description of the PFSP is given as follows: let $\{s_1, s_2, \ldots, s_n\}$ be a set of n jobs and $\{W_1, W_2, \ldots, W_m\}$ be a set of m machines. In PFSP the jobs are processed through m machines such that the order of processing these jobs is the same on all machines. We can summarize the constraints of the problem as follows:

1. The sequence of processing all jobs on each of the machines is same.
2. The job can be processed on one machine at the same time, also each machine can process one job at a time.
3. Jobs have no priority and there is no breakdown of any machine during the jobs process.
4. The processing times are known for all jobs and for every machine.
5. The jobs are independent of each other, and the preparative time of each job is zero.
6. Machines are continuously available over the processing.
7. The processing cannot be interrupted Once the operation starts nil the job has been released by the machine.
8. The setup time is included in the processing time.
9. Jobs are ready to state at time zero.

The notations of the problem are as follows:
n: the number of jobs.
m: the number of machines.
r: the number of objective functions.
$t_{1,j}$: The processing time of the job j in the first machine.
$t_{2,j}$: The processing time of the job j in the second machine.
$C_{i,j}$: The completion time of the job I in the machine j.
We formulate our model as follows:

$$C_{1,1} = t_{1,1} \tag{1}$$

$$C_{i,1} = C_{i-1,1} + t_{i,1}, 2 \le i \le n \tag{2}$$

$$C_{1,j} = C_{1,j-1} + t_{1,j}, 2 \le j \le m \tag{3}$$

$$C_{i,j} = \max\left[C_{i-1,j}, C_{i,j-1}\right] + t_{i,j}, \tag{4}$$

$$2 \le i \le n, 2 \le j \le m \tag{5}$$

In this work, we restrict the study on the 2-machine ($m = 2$) PFSP and the objective is to find the efficient solutions of the problem.

Let $f_1 = max_i(C_{i,2})$ (i.e., makespan) and $f_2 = \sum_i C_{i,2}$, then according to the three-field representation, the problem can be written as follows: $F_2|perm|(f_1, f_2,)$.

4. Proposed algorithms

4.1 Standard algorithms

We combined two multiobjective algorithms with the proposed IP, the first one is a heuristic proposed by Ref. [23] (MOPE) a partial enumeration heuristic and the second is non dominated sorting genetic algorithm (NSGAII) proposed by [24].

4.1.1 MOPE algorithm

The MOPE heuristic is a multiobjective algorithm based on job insertion and using the Pareto dominance concept to choose the partial and complete solutions. The algorithm is described as follows:

MOPE algorithm.

For h = 1 to r do.

Using the dispatching rules to order the jobs to obtain the sequence $s^j = (J_1, \dots, J.)$

Set $s_1^h = (J_1)$, $S_1^h = \{s_1^h\}$ set of partial sequences with one job.

For M = 2-ton do

For all $s_j^h \in S_{M-1}^h$ do

Insert the MTh job s_j^h in the position I and generating a sequence s_j^l with M jobs

Evaluate:

$$f\left(s_j^l\right) = \left(f_1\left(s_j^h\right), f_2\left(s_j^h\right), \dots, f_r\left(s_j^h\right)\right)$$

Find the set S_M^h of efficient partial sequences from the M.| S_{M-1}^h| generated partial sequences.

End phase M. The set S_n^h contains efficient complete sequences.

Construct the union $\cup_{i=1}^r S_n^i$ and calculate the set of efficient solutions as an approximate set of efficient solutions.

4.1.2 MOGA (NSGAII) algorithm

One of the most popular multiobjective genetic algorithms is the NSGAII Algorithm and many engineering applications have been applied to this algorithm [25].

The main feature of NSGAII is the elitism non dominated sorting procedure. Also crowding distance procedure was applied to rank the sorting non dominated solutions. The algorithm is described as follows:

Let P_0 is parent population generated randomly and sorted based on non-domination. Binary tournament selection, crossover, and mutation procedures are used to obtain a child population Q_0 of size N. The generation is continued as follows:

- $R_t = Q_t \cup P_t$
- $F =$ fast nondominating sort $= (\mathcal{F}_1, \mathcal{F}_2, \ldots, \mathcal{F}_2)$ non dominated fronts of R_t
- Until $|P_{t+1}| < N$
- Calculate crowding distance in front $\mathcal{F}_k$
- $P_{t+1} = P_{t+1} + \mathcal{F}_k$, $\mathcal{F}_k$ is the kth non dominated front in the pop
- Sort P_{t+1} in descending order using crowding distance procedure values
- Choose the first N elements of P_{t+1}
- Q_{t+1} obtained from P_{t+1} using mutation, crossover, and selection on P_{t+1} to obtain Q_{t+1}
- $t = t + 1$

The order of two solutions I and j with respect to the crowding distance and the rank by using the following operator:

$i \prec j$ if $(i_{rank} \prec j_{rank})$ or

$$(i_{rank} = j_{rank} \ and \ i_{dist} > j_{dist})$$

5. Proposed IP

The proposed IP is based on the multiobjective variable neighborhood scheduling and the concept of insertion of jobs through the sequence. This procedure can be combined (with some implementation) to any MOSP (single machine problem or PFSP) to improve the approximation set of efficient solutions. We describe the IP in the following steps:

1. Generate a set (Q) of initial solutions either using dispatching rules for heuristic algorithms or randomly (or both methods) for population-based algorithms.

2. Loop the following steps until the stopping criterion is reached.

    a. Choose randomly a solution s from Q, reset Q if empty.

    b. Apply randomly (from a set of neighborhoods) a neighborhood N_r to s, the resulting is a solution $\grave{s}$ (i.e $N_r(s) = \grave{s}$.

c. Apply the function **INS_FUN**($\grave{s}$) to generate a set of efficient solutions.

d. Add the efficient solutions obtained by step c to the set M.

e. Back to step a.

f. Obtain efficient solutions from all solutions in ES.

3. Back to step 2 until the stopping criterion is reached.

4. If the stopping criterion reached, then stop with the approximate set of efficient solutions.

INS_FUN($\grave{s}$) function:

1. Choose k jobs randomly from $\grave{s}$, the remaining partial sequence has n-k jobs.

2. Insert the first job of the chosen jobs on each position of the remaining partial sequence, the resulting is n-k + 1 partial sequences each one has n-k + 1 jobs, and then construct the efficient solutions from these partial sequences.

3. Insert the second job of the chosen jobs on each position of the obtained efficient partial sequence, the resulting is partial sequences each one has n-k + 2 jobs, and so on until the set of complete efficient solutions.

We note that the number of efficient partial sequences increases when the size of the sequence is big and we need to save the computation times of the algorithm, so practically we choose the best p efficient partial sequences, this is done by sorting the sums of objective functions values of each partial sequence in increasing order, then choose the p efficient partial sequences for the next step. The value of p is set to 500 according to experimental results (i.e., If the number of efficient partial sequences exceeds 500, then, we choose only 500 efficient partial sequences for the next step).

We use three kinds of neighborhoods: swap neighborhood, insertion neighborhood, and reversion neighborhood. In the first kind, two jobs are chosen randomly and swapped between these two jobs. In the second kind choose one job randomly and insert it randomly in another position. In the third kind two jobs are chosen randomly then reverse the partial sequence from the first one to the second. The stopping criterion is the maximum CPU time.

6. Proposed algorithms

One of the most accepted results is that a local search is very effective in improving the performance of metaheuristics [26, 27]. In this paper we applied this idea by combining the IS as a local search to the MOPE algorithm, the result is MOPE-IP, and with MOGA, the result is MOGA-IP.

6.1 MOPE-IP algorithm

We summarize the MOPE-IP algorithm as follows:

1. Run the MOPE heuristic and generate the set of efficient solutions ES1.

2. Use the initial set of efficient solutions to run the IP.

3. The result is the approximate set of efficient solutions ES2.

The final approximate set of efficient solutions is the efficient solutions on the union: ES1 ∪ ES2

6.2 MOGA-IP algorithm

1. Set $H_0 = \varnothing$, generate initial populations P_0 of size N as follows:

    a. Use the IP to generate a set of efficient solutions of size k.

    b. If $k < N$, then generate the remaining solutions randomly.

    c. If $k > N$, then choose the N best solution of the generated solutions.

    d. If $k = N$, then use the generated set as the initial population.

2. P_0 is sorted based on non-domination. Binary tournament selection, crossover, and mutation procedures are used to obtain a child population Q_0 of size N. The generation is continuously as follows:

3. $R_t = Q_t \cup P_t \cup H_t$

4. $F =$ fast nondominating sort $= (\mathcal{F}_1, \mathcal{F}_2, \ldots, \mathcal{F}_2)$ non dominated fronts of R_t

5. Use the binary tournament selection procedure to choose two solutions from the front $\mathcal{F}_1$ then use these solutions to apply the IP to generate the approximate set of efficient solution H_t

6. Until $|P_{t+1}| < N$

7. Calculate the crowding distance in $\mathcal{F}_j$

8. $P_{t+1} = P_{t+1} + \mathcal{F}_j$, $\mathcal{F}_j$ is the jet non dominated front in the pop

9. Sort P_{t+1} in descending order using crowding distance procedure values

10. Choose the first N elements of P_{t+1} to obtain Q_{t+1}

11. Q_{t+1} obtained from P_{t+1} using selection, crossover, and mutation on P_{t+1}

12. $t = t + 1$.

7. Performance of the proposed algorithms

7.1 Test problems

The proposed algorithms are tested in 140 2-machine FSPs at different levels, the size of problems ranges from 4 to 10 jobs for small-size problems and 20 to 80 jobs for large-size problems. The processing times for the FSPs were generated randomly and distributed uniformly in the interval [0,100]. The machine is LENOVO, and the algorithms are coded using MATLAB R.2015 and executed on an Intel (R) Core TM (i7) CPU, (2.5) GHz, and (8.00) GB of RAM.

7.2 Parameter setting

The number of iterations (Max Iteration) for the MOGA algorithm is set as follows:
For 4–10 job problems Max Iteration = 150

- For 20–50 jobs problems Max Iteration = 250
- For 60–80 jobs problems Max Iteration = 500

The size of the population (N) setting is as follows:

- For 4–10 jobs problems N = 50
- For 20–50 jobs problems N = 100
- For 60–80 jobs problems N = 100 (**Figures 1** and **2**)

The probability of crossover and the probability of mutation setting is equal to 0.5.
The time for termination condition for IP is set to 5 seconds. We use dispatching rules to generate initial solutions for IP which are: SPT shortest processing time) [28], LPT (longest processing time) [29].

7.3 Performance metric

We use the complete enumeration method (CEM) to calculate the optimal set of efficient solutions. To obtain the approximate set of efficient solutions we use the concept of reference set (RE). It is defined as the efficient solutions on the union of the efficient solutions obtained by the considered algorithms. To compare the algorithms, we use a cardinal measure (Cr) [4], where Cr = C (RE, A) which is the number of efficient solutions in the intersection set RE ∩ A, where A is the algorithm that is needed to measure its performance.

7.4 Comparative results

In this paper, the comparison between the proposed algorithms' performance is as follows: firstly, we compare between MOPE and proposed MOPE_IP secondly between MOGA and proposed MOGA_IP, and finally between the proposed algorithms (MOPE-IP and MOGA-IP). We use the cardinal measure (Cr) as a

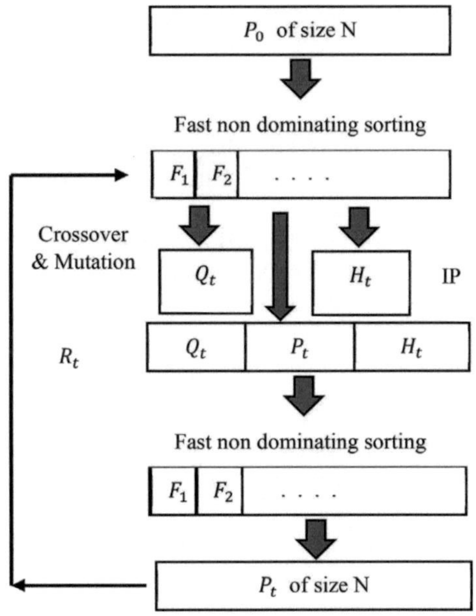

Figure 1.
Graphical representation of MOGA-IP algorithm.

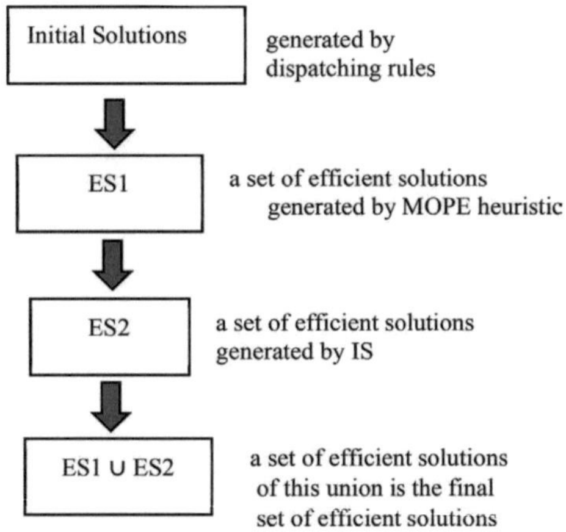

Figure 2.
Graphical representation of MOPE-IP algorithm.

performance metric which calculates the number of efficient solutions obtained by the considered algorithm that belong to the RF set. The RF set collects the efficient solutions for each considered algorithm, and then finds the efficient solutions of the collected solutions, this set can be regarded as an approximate set of efficient solutions. **Table 1** contains the mean values of the Cr measure of the two algorithms MOPE and MOPE-IP, it can be seen that the two algorithms can obtain good results for the given PFSP, also the two algorithms obtain the optimal efficient solutions for small-size problems (i.e., from n = 4 to n = 10 jobs). For the large size problems (i.e., from n = 20 to 80 jobs) (see **Figure 3**), we use the RF set as an approximation set of efficient solutions, it can be seen that the MOPE-IP obtain a better solution than

N	opt	Cr(opt, MOPE)	Cr(opt, MOPE − IP)	Time 1	Time 2
4	2.7	2.7	2.7	0.006	5.01
5	2.8	2.8	2.8	0.017	5.024
6	2.2	2.2	2.2	0.109	5.113
7	2.3	2.3	2.3	0.536	5.541
8	2.2	2.2	2.2	1.011	6.015
9	3	3	3	1.568	6.569
10	2.4	2.4	2.4	2.16	7.165
N	**RF**	**Cr(Ref, MOPE)**	**Cr(RF, MOPE − IP)**	**Time 1**	**Time 2**
20	3	2.2	2.7	11.191	21.22
30	4.1	0.6	1.3	26.376	36.386
40	3.5	1	1.9	47.351	57.356
50	2.8	0.6	1.4	76.153	86.163
60	2.7	1.2	1.7	123.979	134.014
70	4.2	1.5	2.2	168.730	178.745
80	4	1.2	2.1	233.757	243.775

Table 1.
The values of optimal efficient solutions (opt), Cr measure of MOPE, MOPE-IP, and the execution times of the two algorithms (Time 1, Time 2).

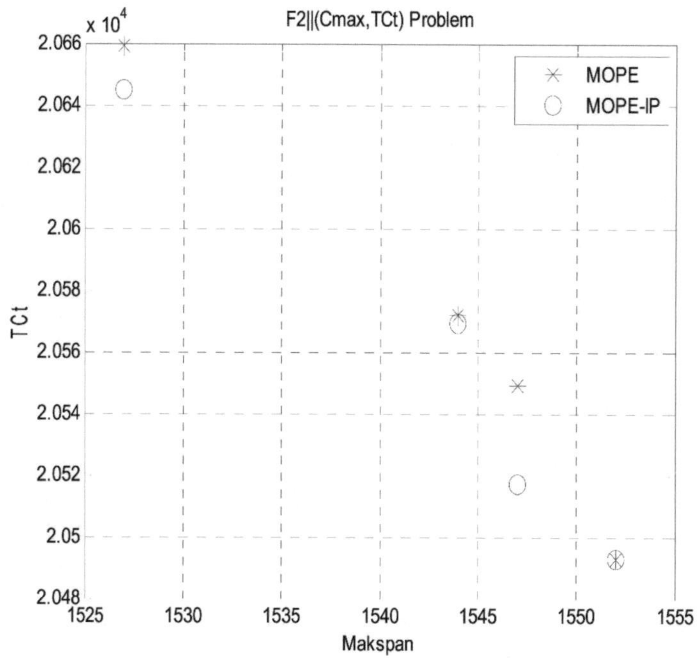

Figure 3.
Efficient solutions for problem F2. (Makspan, TCT) produced by the algorithms MOPE and MOPE-IP for instant of size n = 30.

n	opt	Cr(opt, MOGA)	Cr(opt, MOGA − IP)	Time 1	Time 2
4	2.7	2.7	2.7	25.940	276.649
5	2.8	2.8	2.8	26.369	216.730
6	2.2	2.2	2.2	26.875	124.480
7	2.3	2.1	2.3	26.687	83.311
8	2.2	2	2.2	26.562	61.158
9	3	2.9	3	26.497	55.465
10	2.4	1.7	2.4	27.117	54.773
n	**RF**	**Cr(RF, MOGA)**	**Cr(RF, MOGA − IP)**	**Time 1**	**Time 2**
20	3	0.9	2.3	252.349	298.708
30	4.1	0.6	2.5	254.426	303.963
40	3.5	0.4	1.2	263.3	307.46
50	2.8	0.3	1.1	269.902	316.958
60	2.7	0.3	0.7	295.006	340.23
70	4.2	0	2	277.65	329.781
80	4	0	1.9	283.813	332.473

Table 2.
The values of optimal efficient solutions (opt), Cr measure of MOGA, MOGA-IP, and the execution times of the two algorithms (Time 1, Time 2).

MOPE and most solutions obtained by MOPE dominated by the others obtained by MOPE-IP. **Table 2** contains the mean values of the Cr measure of the two algorithms MOGA and MOGA-IP, it can be seen that the two algorithms can obtain good results- with preference to MOGA-IP- for the given PFSP, also the MOGA-IP algorithm obtains the optimal efficient solutions for small size problems (i.e., from n = 4 to n = 10 jobs). For the large size problems (i.e., from n = 20 to 80 jobs), (see **Figure 4**), it can be seen that the performance of MOGA-IP is better than MOGA. From **Tables 1–3**, it can be seen that most solutions obtained by MOGA-IP dominate the solutions of MOGA. According to the results in **Tables 1** and **3**, it can be seen that the execution time is affected by IP for the two algorithms MOPE-IP and MOGA-IP.

8. Conclusions and future work

There are several methods appear in the literature to develop and improve the performance of metaheuristics algorithms to solve MOSP algorithms by using local search methods, some of them based on the aggregation functions and others based on the Pareto optimal concept to obtain efficient solutions. In this paper we develop a multiobjective procedure based on the VNS and insertion concept of jobs through the sequence proposed by Nawaz et al. [27] to solve a single objective m machine FSP and developed by Ref. [30] for multiobjective problems. Our proposed IP adapted the idea of insertion to MOPE algorithms and MOGA algorithms to solve 2-machine PFSP including two objective functions: makespan and total completion times. For the MOPE-IP algorithm, the MOPE run at first and the algorithm use the obtained

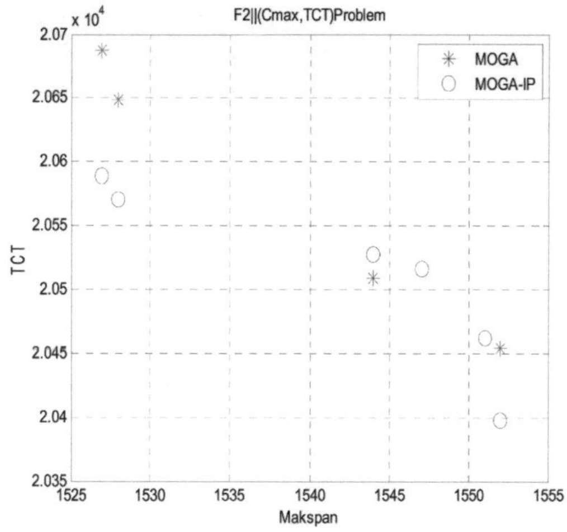

Figure 4.
Efficient solutions for problem F2. (Makspan, TCT) produced by the algorithms MOGA and MOGA-IP for instant of size n = 30.

	Number of efficient solutions				
	Total	**MOPE**	**MOPE − IP**	**MOGA**	**MOGA − IP**
Opt	709	709	709	686	709
RF	546	210	315	74	282

Table 3.
The total number of efficient solutions obtained by the four algorithms MOPE, MOPE-IP, MOGA, and MOGA-IP.

efficient solutions as initial set of efficient solutions for IP, this insures the improvements of the final set of efficient solutions. For MOGA-IP algorithm, the IP adapted such that it uses the obtained efficient solutions at each iteration as initial efficient solutions, this insures the increasing of the diversity of the population search. To save the computational times, the IP runs only three or four times through the algorithm.

Experimental data confirm that the hybrid algorithms give reasonable results compared with the original algorithm, also the proposed IP can improve the performance of the original algorithms. But we note some things:

1. Because of the increasing of computational times of the algorithm, we cannot take all efficient partial sequences in **INS_FUN** procedure, we reduce them to (p = 500) if the number exceeds 500 efficient partial sequences as mentioned above. So, we may lose some complete efficient solutions through this process.

2. Also because of computational times, we cannot examine all neighborhood solutions of the considered (current solution) in the local search steps of the proposed hybrid algorithms, so to ensure the diversity, we choose the neighborhood randomly and we use three kinds of neighborhoods for the current solution.

3. According to the two above points, we need to further improving the IP procedure for choosing reasonable best efficient partial sequences.

4. Further work can be done by applying the proposed IP procedure on other multi-objective algorithms, especially those algorithms that use populations ensemble where it is difficult to produce good solutions and performance can be improved in a relatively short time and with simple implementation so that the insertion work is effective.

Author details

Hafed Motair
Distinguished Secondary School - Diwaniya, Ministry of Education, Iraq

*Address all correspondence to: hafedmotair@gmail.com

References

[1] Pinedo M, Haddadi K. Scheduling: Theory, algorithms and systems development. In: Operations Research Proceedings. Vol. 1992. Jahrestagung: Springer Berlin Heidelberg; 1991. pp. 35-42

[2] Kan AHGR. Machine Scheduling Problems: Classification, Complexity and Computations. Springer Science & Business Media; 2012

[3] Deb K, Jain H. An evolutionary many-objective optimization algorithm using reference-point-based nondominated sorting approach, part I: Solving problems with box constraints. IEEE Transactions on Evolutionary Computation. 2013;**18**(4):577-601

[4] Arroyo JEC, dos Santos Ottone R, de Paiva Oliveira A. Multi-objective variable neighborhood search algorithms for a single machine scheduling problem with distinct due windows. Electronic Notes in Theoretical Computer Science. 2011;**281**:5-19

[5] El-Mihoub TA, Hopgood AA, Nolle L, Battersby A. Hybrid genetic algorithms: A review. Engineering Letters. 2006; **13**(2):124-137

[6] Nagar A, Herbage SS, Haddock J. A combined branch-and-bound and genetic algorithm-based approach for a flowshop scheduling problem. Annals of Operations Research. 1996;**63**(3): 397-414

[7] Murata T, Ishibashi H, Tanaka H. Multi-objective genetic algorithm and its applications to flowshop scheduling. Computers & Industrial Engineering. 1996;**30**(4):957-968

[8] Juszkiewicz A. Genetic local search for multi-objective combinatorial optimization. European Journal of Operational Research. 2002;**137**(1):50-71

[9] Aldowaisan T, Allahverdi A. New heuristics for m-machine no-wait flowshop to minimize total completion time. Omega. 2004;**32**(5):345-352

[10] Reddy BSP, Rao CSP. A hybrid multi-objective GA for simultaneous scheduling of machines and AGVs in FMS. The International Journal of Advanced Manufacturing Technology. 2006;**31**(5–6):602-613

[11] Tavakkoli-Moghaddam R, Rahimi-Vahed A, Mirzaei AH. A hybrid multi-objective immune algorithm for a flow shop scheduling problem with bi-objectives: Weighted mean completion time and weighted mean tardiness. Information Sciences. 2007;**177**(22): 5072-5090

[12] Li B-B, Wang L, Liu B. An effective PSO-based hybrid algorithm for multiobjective permutation flow shop scheduling. IEEE Transactions on Systems, Man, and Cybernetics-Part A: Systems and Humans. 2008;**38**(4):818-831

[13] Sindhya K, Miettinen K, Deb K. A hybrid framework for evolutionary multi-objective optimization. IEEE Transactions on Evolutionary Computation. 2012;**17**(4):495-511

[14] Sadeghi J, Sadeghi S, Niaki STA. A hybrid vendor managed inventory and redundancy allocation optimization problem in supply chain management: An NSGA-II with tuned parameters. Computers & Operations Research. 2014;**41**:53-64

[15] Ghasemi P, Talebi Brijani E. An integrated FAHP-PROMETHEE approach for selecting the best flexible manufacturing system. European Online Journal of Natural and Social Sciences. 2014;**3**(4):1137

[16] Xu L, Yeming J, Ming H. Solving hybrid flow-shop scheduling based on improved multi-objective artificial bee colony algorithm. In: 2016 2nd International Conference on Cloud Computing and Internet of Things (CCIOT). IEEE; 2016. pp. 43-47

[17] Li J, Han Y, Wang C. A hybrid artificial bee colony algorithm to solve multi-objective hybrid flowshop in cloud computing systems. In: International Conference on Cloud Computing and Security. Nanjing, China: Springer International Publishing; 2017. pp. 201-213

[18] Li J, Sang H, Han Y, Wang C, Gao K. Efficient multi-objective optimization algorithm for hybrid flow shop scheduling problems with setup energy consumptions. Journal of Cleaner Production. 2018;**181**:584-598

[19] Liu X, Zhang D. An improved SPEA2 algorithm with local search for multi-objective investment decision-making. Applied Sciences. 2019;**9**(8):1675

[20] de Siqueira EC, Souza MJF, de Souza SR. An MO-GVNS algorithm for solving a multiobjective hybrid flow shop scheduling problem. International Transactions in Operational Research. 2020;**27**(1):614-650

[21] Öztop H, Tasgetiren MF, Eliiyi DT, Pan Q-K, Kandiller L. An energy-efficient permutation flowshop scheduling problem. Expert Systems with Applications. 2020;**150**:113279

[22] Li J et al. Efficient multi-objective algorithm for the lot-streaming hybrid flowshop with variable sub-lots. Swarm and Evolutionary Computation. 2020;**52**: 100600

[23] Arroyo JEC, Armentano VA. A partial enumeration heuristic for multi-objective flowshop scheduling problems. Journal of the Operational Research Society. 2004;**55**(9):1000-1007

[24] Deb K, Agrawal S, Pratap A, Meyarivan T. A fast elitist non-dominated sorting genetic algorithm for multi-objective optimization: NSGA-II. In: International Conference on Parallel Problem Solving from Nature. Paris, France: Springer Berlin Heidelberg; 2000. pp. 849-858

[25] Ghasemi P, Khalili-Damghani K, Hafezalkotob A, Raissi S. Stochastic optimization model for distribution and evacuation planning (a case study of Tehran earthquake). Socio-Economic Planning Sciences. 2020;**71**:100745

[26] Wang L, Shen W. Process Planning and Scheduling for Distributed Manufacturing. Springer Science & Business Media; 2007

[27] Zheng D-Z, Wang L. An effective hybrid heuristic for flow shop scheduling. The International Journal of Advanced Manufacturing Technology. 2003;**21**(1):38-44

[28] Framinan JM, Leisten R, Ruiz-Usano R. Efficient heuristics for flowshop sequencing with the objectives of makespan and flowtime minimisation. European Journal of Operational Research. 2002;**141**(3):559-569

[29] Nawaz M, Enscore EE Jr, Ham I. A heuristic algorithm for the m-machine, n-job flow-shop sequencing problem. Omega. 1983;**11**(1):91-95

[30] Geiger MJ. Randomised variable neighborhood search for multi objective optimization. arXiv preprint arXiv: 0809.0271, 2008

Chapter 5

Agile Circularity: Reactive Scheduling Approaches

Krisztián Attila Bakon

Abstract

Reactive scheduling is essential for optimizing resource flows in the circular economy. This chapter explores agile scheduling strategies that enable real-time adaptation to disruptions and changes, ensuring efficient utilization of materials and minimizing waste. By leveraging dynamic resource allocation and closed-loop systems, organizations can build resilient supply chains capable of responding to evolving market demands and sustainability requirements. Key topics include supply chain agility, sustainable operations management, and material flow optimization techniques tailored for circular business models. The chapter provides practical insights and case studies demonstrating the benefits of reactive scheduling in driving the transition toward a more sustainable, circular future.

Keywords: agile circularity, reactive scheduling, supply chain agility, circular economy, sustainability

1. Introduction

The integration of Agile Circularity and Reactive Scheduling principles has become increasingly relevant in the context of modern production systems due to the growing need for sustainable, flexible, and responsive manufacturing processes. Agile Circularity combines agile methodologies with circular economy principles to establish a production environment that minimizes waste, optimizes resource utilization, and enhances adaptability [1, 2]. Reactive Scheduling, on the other hand, is a strategy that addresses the unpredictability of production environments by real-time adjustment of schedules in response to disruptions [3].

Modern production systems face a high degree of uncertainty driven by factors such as volatile market demands, technological advancements, and evolving environmental regulations. Rapidly changing consumer preferences, global supply chain disruptions, and economic fluctuations can make it challenging to accurately predict and plan for future demand [4, 5]. The pace of technological change, from automation to digitalization, can disrupt traditional production processes and require continuous adaptation [6, 7]. Additionally, evolving environmental policies and sustainability requirements can necessitate changes in production methods and resource utilization [8, 9].

In addition to uncertainty, modern production systems also face various types of disruptions, including equipment failures, supply chain issues, and external shocks such as natural disasters and pandemics. Unexpected breakdowns or malfunctions in

IntechOpen

production equipment can cause delays and disrupt the flow of operations [10, 11]. Disruptions in the supply of raw materials, components, or logistics can lead to production bottlenecks and supply shortages [12]. Events such as natural disasters, pandemics, or other external shocks can severely impact production capabilities and supply networks [13, 14].

Reactive scheduling involves adjusting production schedules in response to unforeseen changes and disruptions. Unlike proactive scheduling, which plans for potential disruptions in advance, reactive scheduling addresses issues as they arise, making it well-suited for dynamic and uncertain environments [10]. Reactive scheduling, which involves making real-time adjustments to production and operations based on current conditions, plays a crucial role in the circular economy. It ensures that resources are used optimally and that production processes are flexible and adaptive to changes in supply and demand. By adjusting schedules based on actual demand and resource availability, companies can minimize overproduction and reduce waste. Reactive scheduling allows for better coordination of repair, reuse, and recycling processes, ensuring that materials and products are kept in use longer. Companies can quickly adapt to disruptions in supply chains, such as shortages of raw materials, by reallocating resources and adjusting production plans.

The integration of Agile Circularity and Reactive Scheduling principles provides a comprehensive approach to addressing the challenges posed by uncertainty and disruptions in modern production systems. By adopting agile methodologies and circular economy principles, organizations can enhance their flexibility, responsiveness, and sustainability [15, 16]. Agile Circularity leverages the iterative and incremental nature of agile methodologies, applying them to the production lifecycle to promote continuous improvement and rapid adaptation [17]. This concept aligns with the circular economy's focus on resource efficiency, waste minimization, and product lifecycle extension.

Simultaneously, the adoption of Reactive Scheduling strategies enables real-time adjustments to production schedules, ensuring operational continuity and resilience in the face of unpredictable events [18, 19]. By combining agile principles with reactive strategies, organizations can create a production environment that is not only environmentally responsible but also highly adaptable to changes and disruptions [20].

This holistic approach empowers organizations to navigate the complex and dynamic production landscape, mitigating the impact of uncertainty and disruptions while fostering a more sustainable and adaptable manufacturing ecosystem. The integration of Agile Circularity and Reactive Scheduling principles offers a comprehensive framework for improving both the sustainability and responsiveness of manufacturing systems, enabling organizations to thrive in the face of modern production challenges.

2. Foundations of circular economy

The circular economy is a model of production and consumption that involves reusing, repairing, refurbishing, and recycling existing materials and products for as long as possible. This approach contrasts sharply with the traditional linear economy, which follows a 'make, use, dispose' pattern. The circular economy aims to reduce waste and environmental impact while enhancing resource efficiency [21, 22]; therefore, it aims to keep products, materials, and resources in use for as long as possible, extracting maximum value from them while in use, then recovering and regenerating products and materials at the end of each service life [23]. Key principles of the circular economy, among others, are:

- Design for longevity: products are designed to last longer, with an emphasis on durability, reparability, and upgradability.
- Maintaining value: keeping products and materials at their highest utility and value at all times through reuse, repair, refurbishing, and recycling.
- Waste elimination: reducing waste to a minimum by closing the loops in industrial ecosystems.
- System effectiveness: improving overall system efficiency by considering the entire lifecycle of products and materials, and the system-wide impacts, such as environmental and social consequences.

Several benefits of adopting the circular economy model can be stated. By reusing and recycling materials, the demand for new raw materials is reduced, preserving natural resources. Manufacturing new products from recycled materials generally consumes less energy compared to producing from virgin resources. Repair, refurbishing, and recycling activities are labor-intensive, leading to the creation of local jobs and skills development. Significant reductions in greenhouse gas emissions and pollution are achieved by minimizing waste and promoting sustainable practices. Circular economy practices can make economies more resilient by reducing dependency on imported raw materials and mitigating the risks associated with resource scarcity.

It goes without saying that implementing a circular economy is not without challenges. Society needs to shift its perception from ownership to stewardship, valuing long-term use over newness. Traditional economic metrics like GDP do not align well with circular economy practices. New metrics that value resource efficiency and waste reduction are needed. Governments need to create policies that incentivize circular practices, such as tax incentives for recycling and penalties for wasteful practices. Continued research and development are essential to create new methods for material recovery, such as de-polymerizing and de-alloying, which can recycle materials at the atomic level.

Several studies have explored reactive scheduling within the context of the circular economy. For instance, literature has highlighted the importance of flexibility and real-time decision-making in achieving sustainable operations [24, 25]. Research has also focused on the integration of reactive scheduling with advanced technologies such as IoT and big data analytics to enhance decision-making capabilities [26].

3. Synergizing agility, sustainability, and efficiency in supply chains

This section delves into critical concepts and practices essential for modern supply chain and operations management. It highlights the importance of agility, sustainability, and material flow optimization in creating efficient and resilient systems. The interconnectedness of these elements is pivotal in advancing toward circular economy goals, where resource efficiency and environmental sustainability are paramount.

3.1 Supply chain agility

Supply chain agility refers to the ability of a supply chain to quickly respond to changes in the market and environment. This agility is crucial for maintaining the circularity of supply chains, where materials and products must be efficiently cycled back into the production process. Supply chain agility is defined as the capability of a supply chain to rapidly respond to market changes and environmental shifts. This agility involves the ability to swiftly adjust operations, supply chain processes, and logistics to meet new demands and challenges [27]. Agility in supply chains is crucial for maintaining competitiveness and customer satisfaction. It allows companies to respond to unexpected disruptions, demand fluctuations, and technological advancements. Circular supply chains aim to minimize waste and make the most of resources by cycling materials back into the production process. This approach supports sustainability and reduces environmental impact [2]. Agility is essential for circular supply chains as it enables the efficient return and reuse of materials. Companies can better handle the complexities of recycling, remanufacturing, and waste management with agile practices [28]. Several frameworks and strategies can enhance supply chain agility, including technology integration, flexible logistics, and collaboration with partners. Embracing digital tools and real-time data analytics is critical for agile operations [29].

3.2 Sustainable operations management

Sustainable operations management focuses on designing and managing operational processes to minimize environmental impact and optimize resource use. This approach integrates principles of sustainability into the core operational strategies and practices [30]. Key principles of sustainable operations management include reducing waste, enhancing energy efficiency, and optimizing the use of natural resources. Strategies such as lean manufacturing, green supply chain management, and life cycle assessment are often employed [31]. Reactive scheduling involves adjusting schedules in real time in response to disruptions and unforeseen changes in the production process. It is critical for maintaining efficiency and minimizing downtime in dynamic environments [10]. Integrating sustainability with reactive scheduling involves creating flexible systems that can adapt to changes while minimizing environmental impact. This includes using renewable energy sources, reducing waste during rescheduling, and optimizing resource allocation [32]. Sustainable operation management supports the goals of the circular economy by promoting the reuse, remanufacturing, and recycling of products and materials. Reactive scheduling can facilitate these processes by efficiently managing the return and reintegration of resources into production cycles [33]. Advancements in technology, such as the Internet of Things (IoT), artificial intelligence (AI), and big data analytics, play a significant role in enhancing sustainable operations and reactive scheduling. These technologies enable better monitoring, decision-making, and optimization of processes [34].

3.3 Material flow optimization

Material flow optimization involves improving the efficiency of the movement of materials within a production system. This optimization is critical in closed-loop systems where materials are recycled and reused, supporting sustainability and reducing waste [35, 36]. Lean manufacturing focuses on minimizing waste and improving efficiency by streamlining production processes. Techniques such as value stream mapping, kaizen, and 5S are used to identify and eliminate non-value-adding activities [37]. Just-in-time production is a strategy that aims to increase efficiency and decrease waste by receiving goods only as they are needed in the production process. This approach reduces inventory costs and improves material flow [38]. Reverse logistics involves the process of moving goods from their typical final destination for the purpose of capturing value or proper disposal. It is a key component of closed-loop supply chains and contributes to sustainability [33]. The integration of lean manufacturing, just-in-time production, and reverse logistics is essential for optimizing material flow in closed-loop systems. These techniques play crucial roles in achieving this optimization. The integration of these techniques, supported by technological advancements, ensures that materials are efficiently used, recycled, and re-entered into the production cycle [39].

4. Methodologies and techniques

In the ever-evolving landscape of production and service environments, the ability to dynamically allocate resources and adjust schedules in real time is paramount. This section briefly explores some potential components of reactive scheduling, including dynamic resource allocation, mathematical models and algorithms, and technological tools. By understanding and integrating these elements, organizations can significantly enhance their operational efficiency, responsiveness, and adaptability to changing conditions.

4.1 Dynamic resource allocation

Dynamic resource allocation in reactive scheduling refers to the real-time adjustment of resources to meet current operational demands and conditions. This approach is essential for dealing with uncertainties and disruptions in production and service environments, ensuring efficiency and responsiveness [40, 41]. Heuristic approaches provide practical solutions to complex scheduling problems through rules and guidelines derived from experience. These methods are often simpler and faster, making them suitable for real-time applications [42]. Metaheuristic approaches, including genetic algorithms and ant colony optimization, are advanced strategies designed to find near-optimal solutions for complex scheduling problems. These methods mimic natural processes to explore and exploit the solution space effectively [43]. Genetic algorithms (GAs) are inspired by the process of natural selection and genetics. They are used to solve optimization problems by evolving a population of solutions over iterations, and applying operations such as selection, crossover, and mutation [44]. Ant colony optimization (ACO) is inspired by the foraging behavior of ants. This technique uses a colony of artificial ants to explore solutions, relying on pheromone trails to guide the search toward optimal or near-optimal solutions [45]. Dynamic resource allocation in reactive scheduling is crucial for adapting to real-time changes and uncertainties. Heuristic and metaheuristic approaches, such as genetic algorithms and ant colony optimization, provide powerful tools for solving these complex problems.

4.2 Mathematical models and algorithms

Mathematical models and algorithms play a critical role in reactive scheduling. Models such as mixed-integer programming (MIP) and constraint satisfaction problems (CSP) are frequently used to represent and solve scheduling issues. Clear and concise mathematical notations should be used to explain these models [40]. Mixed-integer programming is a powerful mathematical modeling technique used to represent scheduling problems. MIP models include both continuous and integer variables, allowing for the precise formulation of complex constraints and objectives [46].

Constraint satisfaction problems involve finding values for variables within specified constraints. CSP models are widely used in scheduling due to their flexibility in handling various types of constraints and objectives [47].

Several algorithms are used to solve MIP and CSP models effectively. These include branch-and-bound, branch-and-cut, and various heuristic and metaheuristic methods [48]. Heuristic and metaheuristic algorithms, such as genetic algorithms, simulated annealing, and ant colony optimization, are often employed to find near-optimal solutions to large and complex scheduling problems [49]. Ongoing research focuses on improving the scalability, robustness, and adaptability of mathematical models and algorithms in reactive scheduling. Advances in computational power and algorithmic techniques continue to enhance their practical applicability [50]. Mathematical models and algorithms are fundamental in reactive scheduling, enabling precise and efficient solutions to complex scheduling problems. Mixed-integer programming and constraint satisfaction problems are prominent models, while various algorithms provide effective tools for solving these models.

4.3 Technological tools

Technological advancements, particularly the Internet of Things (IoT) and cloud-based solutions, have revolutionized reactive scheduling by enabling real-time data collection, analysis, and decision-making. These technologies support efficient resource management and quick adaptation to changes [26, 51]. IoT refers to the network of interconnected devices that collect and exchange data. In reactive scheduling, IoT devices provide real-time monitoring of resources, production processes, and environmental conditions, facilitating timely adjustments to schedules [52]. Cloud-based solutions offer scalable and flexible computing resources that support data storage, processing, and analysis. These solutions enable real-time collaboration and data sharing across different locations, enhancing the responsiveness of scheduling systems [53]. The integration of IoT and cloud computing creates a powerful framework for reactive scheduling. IoT devices collect real-time data, which is then processed and analyzed using cloud-based platforms to support decision-making and resource optimization [54]. Real-time data collection and analysis are critical for reactive scheduling. IoT sensors and cloud-based analytics provide continuous monitoring and instant feedback, allowing for rapid adjustments to schedules and resource allocations [55]. Technological advancements enable quick decision-making by providing real-time insights into production processes and resource availability. This efficiency is crucial for managing disruptions and ensuring optimal use of resources [56]. Future research is likely to focus on enhancing the integration and interoperability of IoT and cloud-based solutions in reactive scheduling. Emerging trends such as edge computing and artificial intelligence will further enhance these systems [57]. Technological advancements such as IoT and cloud-based solutions significantly support reactive scheduling by enabling real-time data collection, analysis, and decision-making. The integration of these technologies enhances the efficiency and responsiveness of scheduling systems, ensuring optimal resource management and quick adaptation to changes.

5. Challenges and solutions

The influence of stochastic variations in consumer demand on the optimization of disaster relief logistics operations underscores the necessity for the implementation of adaptive resource allocation algorithms capable of dynamically adjusting to unpredictable shifts in demand patterns. Disaster operations management requires the development of flexible scheduling systems that can rapidly respond to unforeseen changes in the volume and distribution of relief supply requests from affected populations in order to efficiently allocate limited resources and minimize response times. Incorporating stochastic programming techniques into the design of decision support tools for disaster managers can enhance the resilience of relief supply chains to demand shocks, enabling more effective and equitable distribution of critical supplies in the aftermath of large-scale emergencies and natural disasters [58].

Similarly, the inherent vulnerabilities in complex supply chain networks, such as the risk of disruptions and their cascading effects on production scheduling and distribution, necessitate the development and implementation of proactive risk management strategies to mitigate the potential for operational and financial losses. Disruptions in the supply of raw materials, components, or logistics services can propagate through interconnected supply chains, leading to production delays, inventory shortages, and unfulfilled customer demand. Effective supply chain risk management requires a multifaceted approach that combines risk identification, assessment, mitigation, and contingency planning. This includes strategies such as supplier diversification, inventory optimization, transportation mode flexibility, and the use of advanced analytics to predict and respond to potential disruptions [5]. By adopting a holistic view of supply chain risk and implementing appropriate mitigation measures, organizations can enhance the resilience and responsiveness of their supply chains, ensuring continuity of operations and customer satisfaction in the face of unexpected disruptions.

The operational practices employed in the context of sustainable green supply chain management, including the procurement, processing, and reuse of recyclable materials, face significant challenges related to the limited availability and inconsistent quality of post-consumer waste streams. The transition toward a circular economy model requires the development of effective reverse logistics systems to collect, sort, and reprocess end-of-life products and packaging. However, the lack of standardized collection methods, varying consumer participation rates, and the presence of contaminants in recyclable materials can lead to supply shortages and quality issues for manufacturers seeking to incorporate recycled content into their products. Addressing these challenges necessitates a collaborative approach among stakeholders, including policymakers, waste management authorities, producers, and consumers, to establish a robust collection infrastructure, improve recycling education and participation, and incentivize the use of recycled materials in manufacturing processes. Technological advancements in sorting, cleaning, and reprocessing technologies can also help to increase the availability and quality of recyclable materials, enabling more efficient and cost-effective green supply chain operations. By overcoming the barriers related to recyclable material supply, organizations can enhance the sustainability of their supply chains, reduce waste, and contribute to the transition toward a more circular and resource-efficient economy [59].

The dynamic allocation of resources in real time to optimize operational efficiency is a complex task that necessitates the implementation of advanced optimization algorithms and the integration of real-time data streams from various sources. Resource allocation problems in dynamic environments involve making decisions under uncertainty, where the availability and demand for resources can change rapidly based on evolving conditions. Addressing these challenges requires the development of intelligent decision support systems that can process large volumes of data, model complex interdependencies, and generate optimal resource allocation plans in near real time. These systems typically employ techniques such as stochastic programming, robust optimization, and machine learning to handle uncertainty, capture nonlinearities, and adapt to changing circumstances. The integration of real-time data from sensors, enterprise systems, and external sources enables these algorithms to make informed decisions based on the current state of the system and anticipate future needs. By leveraging computational power and advanced analytics, organizations can achieve more efficient and responsive resource allocation, leading to improved operational performance, reduced costs, and enhanced customer satisfaction in dynamic environments [60].

The persistent problem of data silos, characterized by the segregation of data within isolated information systems and organizational units, can impede effective communication, decision-making, and business-IT alignment, leading to challenges in efficient scheduling and resource allocation. Data silos arise due to various factors, such as the use of disparate legacy systems, lack of data governance policies, and organizational culture that prioritizes functional autonomy over enterprise-wide collaboration. The lack of data integration and interoperability across these silos can result in inconsistent, incomplete, or outdated information being used for decision-making, leading to suboptimal outcomes. In the context of scheduling, the absence of a unified view of resource availability, demand, and constraints can lead to scheduling conflicts, inefficient resource utilization, and missed deadlines. Addressing the data silo problem requires a multifaceted approach that combines technological solutions, such as enterprise application integration, data warehousing, and master data management, with organizational changes, such as the establishment of data governance frameworks, cross-functional collaboration, and the promotion of a data-driven culture. By breaking down data silos and fostering a culture of data sharing and integration, organizations can enhance business-IT alignment, improve decision-making, and optimize scheduling processes, ultimately leading to increased operational efficiency and competitive advantage [61].

The multifaceted factors influencing the adoption and diffusion of new scheduling technologies across different countries and industries can provide valuable insights into the barriers faced by firms in implementing innovative solutions to optimize resource allocation and improve operational efficiency. Technology adoption is a complex process that is influenced by a combination of technological, organizational, and environmental factors. Technological factors include the perceived complexity, compatibility, and relative advantage of the new technology compared to existing practices. Organizational factors encompass the firm's size, structure, culture, and the support of top management. Environmental factors pertain to the competitive pressure, regulatory environment, and the availability of technological infrastructure and skilled labor. Resistance to adopting new scheduling technologies can stem from a variety of these factors, such as the perceived high costs of implementation and maintenance, the complexity of integrating new systems with existing legacy platforms, and the inertia of organizational routines and practices. Cross-country comparisons can reveal how these factors vary based on the level of economic development, cultural norms, and institutional frameworks. Understanding these factors can help policymakers and industry leaders develop targeted strategies to promote technology adoption, such as providing financial incentives, improving technological infrastructure, and fostering a culture of innovation and continuous improvement. By overcoming the barriers to technology adoption, firms can enhance their competitive advantage and contribute to the overall productivity and resilience of their respective industries and economies [62].

The ability to seamlessly scale computing resources to accommodate increasing and diverse demands is a critical performance attribute of cloud-based services and a significant technological challenge in the design of robust and efficient scheduling systems. As the volume and complexity of workloads grow, cloud platforms must dynamically provision and allocate resources, such as virtual machines, storage, and network bandwidth, to ensure that service level agreements are met without over-provisioning or under-provisioning resources. This requires the implementation of intelligent resource management algorithms that can accurately predict future demand, optimize resource utilization, and rapidly scale resources up or down based on changing conditions. Failure to achieve scalability can lead to performance degradation, service interruptions, and customer dissatisfaction. Similarly, in the context of scheduling systems, the ability to handle a large number of tasks, resources, and constraints while maintaining low latency and high throughput is essential for meeting the demands of modern business environments. Scheduling algorithms must be designed with scalability in mind, leveraging techniques such as parallel processing, distributed computing, and efficient data structures to handle increasing workloads. The adoption of cloud-native architectures and containerization can further enhance the scalability of scheduling systems by enabling the deployment of microservices and the dynamic scaling of individual components based on demand. By prioritizing scalability in the design and implementation of cloud services and scheduling systems, organizations can ensure that their computing infrastructure and decision support tools remain resilient and responsive to the ever-changing needs of their stakeholders [63].

6. Emerging trends and future directions

Reactive scheduling and agile circularity have emerged as critical strategies for enhancing the efficiency and resilience of modern supply chain management. In the face of increasing complexity, volatility, and disruptions, organizations must adapt their scheduling practices to be more responsive, flexible, and data-driven. This section explores the key advancements and technologies that are enabling the transformation toward reactive scheduling and agile circularity in supply chain management.

6.1 Integration of the Internet of Things

The integration of Internet of Things (IoT) devices has shown significant potential in enhancing the efficiency and responsiveness of scheduling systems. IoT devices enable real-time data collection and monitoring of production processes, resource tracking, and predictive maintenance, thereby improving the accuracy and optimization of scheduling algorithms. The application of IoT in smart cities has demonstrated how real-time data acquisition and monitoring can enhance various operational processes, including scheduling optimization [64]. The implementation of IoT technologies has shown promising results in promoting the circular economy by optimizing resource utilization and monitoring material flows. IoT-based applications in the circular economy include monitoring resource flows, optimizing material usage, and ensuring sustainability by tracking the lifecycle of products and materials. These applications leverage the capabilities of IoT devices to collect and analyze data, enabling informed decision-making and the implementation of sustainable practices in the circular economy [65].

The article [66] presents a case study of a large paint manufacturing company in the Pearl River Delta region of China that integrated IoT and cloud manufacturing technologies to manage its production logistics. The study highlights the significant benefits of adopting a data-driven approach to reactive scheduling in a circular economy context. Key outcomes of the integration include improved warehouse space and forklift utilization rates, reduced logistics waiting costs and overtime working hours by 50%, and an enhanced delivery rate of finished products by up to 50%. The case study emphasizes the importance of real-time monitoring and dynamic adjustments to the logistics process enabled by IoT devices and cloud platforms. Additionally, the optimization of external resource integration, such as public warehouses and rented forklifts, based on real-time demand led to cost savings. The system's ability to adapt to real-time execution dynamics resulted in overall efficiency gains in the logistics process. This comprehensive integration of big data analytics, IoT, and cloud manufacturing demonstrates the significant benefits of a data-driven approach to reactive scheduling in a circular economy context, ensuring more efficient and resilient logistics operations that support sustainable business practices.

6.2 Cloud-based scheduling solutions

Cloud-based scheduling platforms leverage the scalability, flexibility, and cost-effectiveness of cloud computing to optimize resource allocation and task management [53]. By harnessing the power of distributed computing resources, these platforms can adapt to fluctuating demands and provide ubiquitous access to scheduling data and functionalities. However, the adoption of cloud-based scheduling solutions requires careful consideration of data security measures, seamless integration with existing IT infrastructure, and the implementation of robust performance monitoring mechanisms to ensure reliable and consistent service delivery [67].

The article [68] provides a comprehensive analysis of cloud computing, elucidating its definition, advantages, obstacles, and opportunities. The authors define cloud computing as applications delivered as services over the Internet, facilitated by hardware and software in data centers, characterized by the appearance of infinite computing resources on demand, elimination of up-front commitment, and pay-as-you-go pricing. The advantages of cloud computing, such as elasticity to quickly scale resources up or down based on demand, the ability to avoid over- or under-provisioning resources, economies of scale from very large data centers, and higher utilization by multiplexing workloads from different organizations, could potentially translate to benefits for scheduling applications. However, the paper also identifies obstacles, including availability, data lock-in, performance unpredictability, and scalable storage, while suggesting opportunities to overcome these challenges, such as using multiple cloud providers, standardizing application programming interfaces, improving virtual machine support, and inventing scalable storage. The elasticity and scalability of cloud computing could be advantageous for agile development methodologies and reactive scheduling approaches that require rapid adaptation to changing requirements and real-time events. The pay-as-you-go pricing model aligns well with agile practices that deliver software incrementally and enables experimenting with new ideas without large capital outlays, which could also benefit reactive scheduling by only paying for the compute power required to handle current workloads. Additionally, the ability to multiplex workloads from different organizations could provide a more cost-effective infrastructure for running agile development pipelines and reactive scheduling systems compared to dedicated on-premises resources.

6.3 Impact of Big Data analytics

The application of Big Data analytics to scheduling processes can significantly enhance accuracy and efficiency by leveraging the extraction of insights from large and complex datasets. The transformative potential of Big Data analytics across various industries has been well-documented, particularly in its ability to optimize decision-making processes and uncover hidden patterns that inform scheduling practices [69]. Data-driven decision-making is a fundamental aspect of effective scheduling, enabling organizations to respond swiftly to changes in demand and optimize the allocation of resources based on data-driven insights. The synergistic relationship between data science and big data analytics underscores the importance of embracing data-driven approaches to scheduling in order to achieve optimal performance and adaptability in dynamic business environments [70].

The article [71] highlights the significant transformation of supply chain management (SCM) through the integration of Big Data analytics (BDA). Companies that utilize data-driven decision-making outperform their competitors in terms of productivity and profitability. BDA enables the handling of extensive datasets, leading to more precise and insightful decisions in SCM. The combination of data science, predictive analytics, and Big Data can optimize supply chain dynamics, enhancing operational efficiency and competitiveness. Big Data plays a crucial role in scheduling by providing real-time insights and predictive capabilities. In logistics, Big Data can optimize routing by considering various factors such as weather, traffic, and driver characteristics. Predictive analytics helps in anticipating transportation requirements, leading to better scheduling and resource allocation. By integrating consumer sentiment data, businesses can respond promptly to market demands reactively, ensuring timely and efficient scheduling. Data-driven decision-making is central to leveraging Big Data in SCM. It involves using quantitative and qualitative data to make informed decisions that enhance supply chain performance. This approach reduces internal transaction costs, adjusts to supply chain environmental changes, and manages day-to-day operations more effectively. The ability to predict outcomes and understand complex relationships within the supply chain fosters agile circularity, allowing organizations to quickly adapt to changes and improve their reactive scheduling capabilities. The integration of Big Data analytics contributes significantly to reactive scheduling and agile circularity in supply chain management. Big Data enables reactive scheduling by providing real-time data and predictive insights, allowing companies to swiftly adjust their schedules in response to unexpected changes. Agile circularity is enhanced through the integration of Big Data, enabling continuous feedback loops and iterative improvements. This flexibility ensures that supply chains can adapt to market dynamics and consumer demands efficiently.

6.4 Advancements in artificial intelligence and machine learning

The integration of artificial intelligence (AI) and machine learning (ML) algorithms into scheduling systems has the potential to significantly enhance overall efficiency and responsiveness by enabling dynamic optimization and proactive disruption prediction. The application of AI and ML techniques in the context of maintenance has demonstrated their effectiveness in facilitating proactive decision-making and reactive scheduling, thereby minimizing downtime and optimizing resource allocation [56]. Furthermore, the implementation of AI/ML-driven applications in scheduling for sustainable operations encompasses a wide range of functionalities, such as predictive maintenance, demand forecasting, and resource optimization. These practical applications of AI and ML in manufacturing settings have been shown to play a crucial role in enhancing scheduling and operational efficiency, ultimately leading to improved productivity and cost savings [72].

The article [73] explores advancements in AI and ML, highlighting their application in business contexts, which can be particularly useful in reactive scheduling and agile circularity. The authors emphasize that AI, through cognitive technologies, can significantly enhance business processes by automating tasks, generating cognitive insights, and engaging with customers and employees. AI and ML contribute to reactive scheduling by automating complex decision-making processes and providing real-time insights. For instance, AI systems can optimize logistics and supply chain operations by predicting demand, adjusting schedules in response to real-time data, and managing resources more effectively. This capability ensures that businesses can swiftly adapt to changes and unexpected disruptions, thereby maintaining operational efficiency. Moreover, the integration of AI in business processes supports agile circularity. Cognitive technologies enable continuous improvement and adaptation through iterative feedback loops. By leveraging AI for tasks such as predictive maintenance, inventory management, and customer engagement, companies can enhance their responsiveness and flexibility, leading to more sustainable and efficient operations.

6.5 Collaborative platforms and blockchain technology

Collaborative platforms have emerged as a key enabler in enhancing communication and coordination across supply chain networks, leading to more effective and efficient scheduling practices. The transition from cloud computing to cloud manufacturing has highlighted the critical role of collaborative platforms in facilitating real-time data sharing, decision-making, and optimization of scheduling processes [74]. Furthermore, the integration of blockchain technology into scheduling systems has the potential to provide unprecedented levels of transparency and traceability, reducing inefficiencies and ensuring accountability throughout the resource allocation process. The application of blockchain in sustainable supply chain management has been recognized for its ability to enhance transparency, traceability, and trust, which are essential attributes for effective scheduling and resource optimization in dynamic and complex supply chain environments [75].

The article [76] examines how integrating digital supply chains (DSC) with blockchain technology enhances collaborative platforms and ensures transparency. Blockchain offers a decentralized, secure, and transparent system for recording transactions, which significantly improves supply chain interoperability and efficiency. By enabling real-time visibility and traceability of goods and services, blockchain fosters enhanced collaboration among stakeholders. Its public ledger system ensures that all participants have access to the same information, reducing discrepancies and building trust. In collaborative scheduling platforms, blockchain technology facilitates automation and secure sharing of scheduling information through smart contracts, which automatically execute agreements when predefined conditions are met. This streamlines scheduling processes, ensuring adherence to timelines without manual intervention and maintaining data integrity. Furthermore, blockchain enhances supply chain transparency by providing a tamper-proof record of transactions, where each transaction is linked to previous ones, forming an immutable chain. This visibility prevents fraud and unauthorized alterations, with public key infrastructure encrypting and decrypting transaction data for added security. Blockchain's integration in DSC supports reactive scheduling and agile circularity by enabling real-time data sharing and transparency, allowing organizations to quickly adjust schedules in response to disruptions or changes in demand. This adaptability is vital for maintaining supply chain resilience and efficiency. Additionally, blockchain promotes agile circularity by enabling continuous feedback loops and iterative improvements, ensuring documented and traceable changes for better decision-making and adaptive strategies.

6.6 Predictive maintenance integration

The integration of predictive maintenance techniques with scheduling systems can significantly enhance operational efficiency and prevent disruptions by anticipating equipment failures and proactively scheduling maintenance activities accordingly. The application of intelligent prognostics and e-maintenance tools has been instrumental in enabling predictive maintenance strategies, which leverage advanced data analytics and machine learning algorithms to forecast equipment health and remaining useful life. By seamlessly integrating these predictive maintenance capabilities with scheduling systems, organizations can optimize resource allocation, minimize downtime, and ensure the reliability of critical assets, ultimately leading to improved overall equipment effectiveness and cost savings [77].

The article [78] focuses on the application of AI-based predictive maintenance (PdM) techniques for water injection pumps (WIPs) in the oil and gas industry. PdM leverages data-driven insights to optimize maintenance activities, enabling proactive interventions to anticipate and address potential issues before they escalate into significant failures. The review examines the advancements in AI-based PdM models for WIPs, as well as the challenges associated with their implementation. Key PdM techniques discussed include ongoing condition monitoring, failure mode analysis, and statistical analysis to detect abnormalities and identify trends. The increasing availability of data from digitalization and IoT technologies has facilitated the application of advanced analytics, ML and AI in PdM for WIPs. The insights gained from AI-based PdM models for WIPs could potentially contribute to the areas in the context of maintenance scheduling and optimization. By accurately predicting equipment failures and estimating remaining useful life, AI-based PdM models can enable more efficient and responsive maintenance scheduling, aligning with the principles of reactive scheduling. Additionally, the continuous monitoring and optimization of maintenance activities facilitated by AI-based PdM models could contribute to the agile circularity of maintenance processes, allowing for rapid adaptation to changing conditions and continuous improvement. However, further research is needed to establish a more direct connection between AI-based PdM for WIPs and its specific applications in reactive scheduling and agile circularity within the oil and gas industry.

7. Conclusions

In this chapter, we have delved into the intricacies of agile circularity and the imperative role of reactive scheduling in optimizing resource flows within the circular economy. The detailed analysis and discussions presented underscore the necessity of real-time adaptability in scheduling to cope with disruptions and fluctuating market demands. This adaptability ensures the efficient utilization of materials and significantly reduces waste, aligning with the broader goals of sustainability.

Agile circularity is characterized by the ability to swiftly adapt to changes, ensuring that resource flows are continuously optimized. The integration of dynamic resource allocation and closed-loop systems emerges as a cornerstone for developing resilient supply chains. These systems enable organizations to respond promptly and effectively to unexpected changes, thereby maintaining operational efficiency and sustainability. The case studies and practical insights shared in this chapter illustrate the tangible benefits of these strategies, providing a roadmap for businesses aiming to transition toward sustainable, circular business models.

We have touched upon key themes such as supply chain agility, sustainable operations management, and material flow optimization. The findings highlight that reactive scheduling, as a crucial component of agile circularity, not only supports environmental objectives but also enhances economic viability by reducing costs associated with resource inefficiencies and wastage.

Furthermore, the research emphasizes the need for continuous innovation in scheduling methodologies to address emerging challenges in the circular economy. The potential for advancements in technology and data analytics to further refine these methodologies presents exciting opportunities for future research and application.

In conclusion, the shift toward a circular economy is fundamentally linked to the ability to manage resources dynamically and efficiently. Agile circularity, enabled by reactive scheduling, serves as a critical enabler in this transition, fostering sustainability while ensuring that businesses remain competitive and resilient. As industries increasingly embrace circular principles, the insights and strategies discussed in this chapter will be invaluable in guiding their journey toward a more sustainable future.

Acknowledgements

The author acknowledges the use of AI-assisted tools for language polishing of the manuscript.

Author details

Krisztián Attila Bakon
Department of Applied Informatics, Faculty of Information Technology, University Center for Circular Economy Nagykanizsa, University of Pannonia, Nagykanizsa, Hungary

*Address all correspondence to: bakon.krisztian@pen.uni-pannon.hu

References

[1] de Padua Pieroni M, McAloone T, Pigosso D. Business model innovation for circular economy: Integrating literature and practice into a conceptual process model. Proceedings of the Design Society: International Conference on Engineering Design. 2019;**1**(1):2517-2526

[2] Genovese A, Acquaye AA, Figueroa A, Lenny Koh SC. Sustainable supply chain management and the transition towards a circular economy: Evidence and some applications. Omega. 2017;**66**:344-357. New Research Frontiers in Sustainability

[3] Hassan LK, Santos BF, Vink J. Airline disruption management: A literature review and practical challenges. Computers and Operations Research. 2021;**127**:105137

[4] Ivanov BSD, Dolgui A, Ivanova M. Literature review on disruption recovery in the supply chain*. International Journal of Production Research. 2017;**55**(20):6158-6174

[5] Tang CS. Perspectives in supply chain risk management. International Journal of Production Economics. 2006;**103**(2):451-488

[6] Kagermann H, Helbig J, Hellinger A, Wahlster W. Recommendations for Implementing the Trategic Initiative INDUSTRIE 4.0: Securing the Future of German Manufacturing Industry; Final Report of the Industrie 4.0 Working Group. Munich: Forschungsunion; 2013

[7] Frank AG, Dalenogare LS, Ayala NF. Industry 4.0 technologies: Implementation patterns in manufacturing companies. International Journal of Production Economics. 2019;**210**:15-26

[8] Chiaroni D, Chiesa V, Frattini F. The open innovation journey: How firms dynamically implement the emerging innovation management paradigm. Technovation. 2011;**31**(1):34-43. Open Innovation—ISPIM Selected Papers

[9] Lacy P, Rutqvist J. Waste to Wealth: The Circular Economy Advantage. London: Palgrave Macmillan; 2016

[10] Vieira GE, Herrmann JW, Lin E. Rescheduling manufacturing systems: A framework of strategies, policies, and methods. Journal of Scheduling. 2003;**6**:39-62

[11] Ghadge A, Merve ER, Moradlou H, Goswami M. The impact of industry 4.0 implementation on supply chains. Journal of Manufacturing Technology Management. 2020;**31**(4)

[12] Sheffi Y. The Resilient Enterprise: Overcoming Vulnerability for Competitive Advantage. Vol. 1. Cambridge, Massachusetts: The MIT Press; 2005

[13] Ivanov D, Dolgui A. Or-methods for coping with the ripple effect in supply chains during covid-19 pandemic: Managerial insights and research implications. International Journal of Production Economics. 2021;**232**:107921

[14] Craighead CW, Blackhurst J, Rungtusanatham MJ, Handfield RB. The severity of supply chain disruptions: Design characteristics and mitigation capabilities. Decision Sciences. 2007;**38**(1):131-156

[15] Kristoffersen E, Blomsma F, Mikalef P, Li J. The smart circular economy: A digital-enabled circular strategies framework for manufacturing

companies. Journal of Business Research. 2020;**120**:241-261

[16] Nancy CB, Bocken MP, de Pauw I, van der Grinten B. Product design and business model strategies for a circular economy. Journal of Industrial and Production Engineering. 2016;**33**(5):308-320

[17] Geissdoerfer M, Morioka SN, de Carvalho MM, Evans S. Business models and supply chains for the circular economy. Journal of Cleaner Production. 2018;**190**:712-721

[18] Ouelhadj D, Petrovic S. A survey of dynamic scheduling in manufacturing systems. Journal of Scheduling. 2009;**12**(4):417-431

[19] Bakon K, Holczinger T, Süle Z, Jaskó S, Abonyi J. Scheduling under uncertainty for industry 4.0 and 5.0. IEEE Access. 2022;**10**:74977-75017

[20] Batista PSL, Bourlakis M, Maull R. In search of a circular supply chain archetype—A content-analysis-based literature review. Production Planning and Control. 2018;**29**(6):438-451

[21] Geissdoerfer M, Savaget P, Bocken NMP, Hultink EJ. The circular economy—A new sustainability paradigm? Journal of Cleaner Production. 2017;**143**:757-768

[22] Kirchherr J, Reike D, Hekkert M. Conceptualizing the circular economy: An analysis of 114 definitions. Resources, Conservation and Recycling. 2017;**127**:221-232

[23] Walter RS. The circular economy. Nature. 2016;**531**(7595):435-438

[24] Kurbel KE et al. Enterprise Resource Planning and Supply Chain Management. Functions, Business Processes and Software for Manufacturing Companies. Progress in IS. Dordrecht: Springer; 2013

[25] Leal JM, Pompidou S, Charbuillet C, Perry N. Design for and from recycling: A circular ecodesign approach to improve the circular economy. Sustainability. 2020;**12**(23)

[26] Mourtzis D, Panopoulos N, Angelopoulos J. Chapter 5—Production management guided by industrial Internet of Things and adaptive scheduling in smart factories. In: Mourtzis D, editor. Design and Operation of Production Networks for Mass Personalization in the Era of Cloud Technology. Amsterdam, Netherlands: Elsevier; 2022. pp. 117-152

[27] Yusuf YY, Gunasekaran A, Adeleye EO, Sivayoganathan K. Agile supply chain capabilities: Determinants of competitive objectives. European Journal of Operational Research. 2004;**159**(2):379-392. Supply Chain Management: Theory and Applications

[28] Trivellas P, Malindretos G, Reklitis P. Implications of green logistics management on sustainable business and supply chain performance: Evidence from a survey in the Greek agri-food sector. Sustainability. 2020;**12**(24)

[29] Dubey R, Gunasekaran A, Childe SJ, Papadopoulos T, Wamba SF. World class sustainable supply chain management: Critical review and further research directions. The International Journal of Logistics Management. 2017;**28**(2):332-362

[30] Kleindorfer PR, Singhal K, Van Wassenhove LN. Sustainable operations management. Production and Operations Management. 2005;**14**(4):482-492

[31] Pagell M, Zhaohui WU. Building a more complete theory of sustainable supply chain management using case studies of 10 exemplars. Journal of Supply Chain Management. 2009;**45**(2):37-56

[32] Gholami R, Sulaiman AB, Ramayah T, Molla A. Senior managers' perception on green information systems (is) adoption and environmental performance: Results from a field survey. Information and Management. 2013;**50**(7):431-438

[33] Govindan K, Soleimani H, Kannan D. Reverse logistics and closed-loop supply chain: A comprehensive review to explore the future. European Journal of Operational Research. 2015;**240**(3):603-626

[34] Borgia E. The Internet of Things vision: Key features, applications and open issues. Computer Communications. 2014;**54**:1-31

[35] Daniel V, Guide R, Van Wassenhove LN. Or forum–the evolution of closed-loop supply chain research. Operations Research. 2009;**57**(1):10-18

[36] Mujkić Z, Qorri A, Kraslawski A. Sustainability and optimization of supply chains: A literature review. Operations and Supply Chain Management: An International Journal. 2018;**11**:186-199

[37] Bhamu J, Sangwan KS. Lean manufacturing: Literature review and research issues. International Journal of Operations and Production Management. 2014;**34**(7):876-940

[38] Shah R, Ward PT. Lean manufacturing: Context, practice bundles, and performance. Journal of Operations Management. 2003;**21**(2):129-149

[39] Mollenkopf D, Stolze H, Tate WL, Ueltschy M. Green, lean, and global supply chains. International Journal of Physical Distribution and Logistics Management. 2010;**40**(1/2):14-41

[40] Pinedo ML. Scheduling: Theory, Algorithms, and Systems. Cham: Springer; 2022

[41] Pinedo ML. Design and Implementation of Scheduling Systems: More Advanced Concepts. Cham: Springer International Publishing; 2016. pp. 485-508

[42] Jensen MT. Generating robust and flexible job shop schedules using genetic algorithms. IEEE Transactions on Evolutionary Computation. 2003;**7**(3):275-288

[43] Blum C, Roli A. Metaheuristics in combinatorial optimization: Overview and conceptual comparison. ACM Computing Surveys. 2003;**35**(3):268-308

[44] Holland JH. Genetic algorithms. Scientific American. 1992;**267**(1):66-73

[45] Dorigo M. Ant colony optimization. Scholarpedia. 2007;**2**(3):1461. revision #90969

[46] Wolsey LA, Nemhauser GL. Integer and Combinatorial Optimization. Hoboken, New Jersey, U.S.: John Wiley and Sons; 2014

[47] Dechter R. Constraint Processing. Cambridge, Massachusetts, U.S.: Morgan Kaufmann; 2003

[48] Achterberg T. Scip: Solving constraint integer programs. Mathematical Programming Computation. 2009;**1**(1):1-41

[49] Talbi E-G. Metaheuristics: From Design to Implementation. Hoboken, New Jersey, U.S.: John Wiley and Sons; 2009

[50] Hooker JN et al. Integrated Methods for Optimization. Vol. 100. New York City: Springer; 2007

[51] Lee I, Lee K. The Internet of Things (IoT): Applications, investments, and challenges for enterprises. Business Horizons. 2015;**58**(4):431-440

[52] Da Xu L, He W, Li S. Internet of Things in industries: A survey. IEEE Transactions on Industrial Informatics. 2014;**10**(4):2233-2243

[53] Buyya R, Yeo CS, Venugopal S, Broberg J, Brandic I. Cloud computing and emerging it platforms: Vision, hype, and reality for delivering computing as the 5th utility. Future Generation Computer Systems. 2009;**25**(6):599-616

[54] Botta A, de Donato W, Persico V, Pescapé A. Integration of cloud computing and Internet of Things: A survey. Future Generation Computer Systems. 2016;**56**:684-700

[55] Gubbi J, Buyya R, Marusic S, Palaniswami M. Internet of Things (IoT): A vision, architectural elements, and future directions. Future Generation Computer Systems. 2013;**29**(7):1645-1660. Including Special Sections: Cyber-Enabled Distributed Computing for Ubiquitous Cloud and Network Services and Cloud Computing and Scientific Applications–Big Data, Scalable Analytics, and Beyond

[56] Bousdekis A, Magoutas B, Apostolou D, Mentzas G. A proactive decision making framework for condition-based maintenance. Industrial Management and Data Systems. 2015;**115**(7):1225-1250

[57] Shi W, Cao J, Zhang Q, Li Y, Lanyu X. Edge computing: Vision and challenges. IEEE Internet of Things Journal. 2016;**3**(5):637-646

[58] Altay N, Green W III. Or/ms research in disaster operations management. European Journal of Operational Research. 2006;**175**:475-493

[59] Zhu Q, Sarkis J. Relationships between operational practices and performance among early adopters of green supply chain management practices in Chinese manufacturing enterprises. Journal of Operations Management. 2004;**22**(3):265-289

[60] Pinedo ML. Scheduling. Vol. 29. New York City: Springer; 2012

[61] Gilbert Silvius AJ, De Waal B, Smit J. Business and it alignment; answers and remaining questions. In: Pacific Asia Conference on Information Systems, Hyderabad, India. PACIS 2009 PROCEEDINGS. 2009

[62] Kevin Z, Kraemer K, Sean X. The process of innovation assimilation by firms in different countries: A technology diffusion perspective on e-business. Management Science. 2006;**52**:1557-1576

[63] Mohammed M, Batarfi O. Cloud scalability considerations. International Journal of Computer Science and Engineering Survey. 2014;**5**:37-47

[64] Zanella A, Bui N, Castellani A, Vangelista L, Zorzi M. Internet of Things for smart cities. IEEE Internet of Things Journal. 2014;**1**(1):22-32

[65] Pagoropoulos A, Pigosso DCA, McAloone TC. The emergent role of digital technologies in the circular economy: A review. Procedia CIRP. 2017;**64**:19-24. 9th CIRP IPSS Conference: Circular Perspectives on PSS

[66] Qu T, Lei SP, Wang ZZ, Nie DX, Chen X, Huang GQ. Iot-based real-time production logistics synchronization system under smart cloud

manufacturing. The International Journal of Advanced Manufacturing Technology. 2016;**84**(1):147-164

[67] Marston S, Li Z, Bandyopadhyay S, Zhang J, Ghalsasi A. Cloud computing—The business perspective. Decision Support Systems. 2011;**51**(1):176-189

[68] Armbrust M, Fox A, Griffith R, Joseph AD, Katz R, Konwinski A, et al. A view of cloud computing. Communications of the ACM. 2010;**53**(4):50-58

[69] Manyika J, Chui M, Brown B, Bughin J, Dobbs R, Roxburgh C, et al. Big Data: The Next Frontier for Innovation, Competition, and Productivity. New York City: McKinsey and Company; 2011

[70] Provost F, Fawcett T. Data science and its relationship to big data and data-driven decision making. Big Data. 2013;**1**(1):51-59

[71] Waller MA, Fawcett SE. Data science, predictive analytics, and big data: A revolution that will transform supply chain design and management. Journal of Business Logistics. 2013;**34**(2):77-84

[72] Lee J, Bagheri B, Kao H-A. A cyber-physical systems architecture for industry 4.0-based manufacturing systems. Manufacturing Letters. 2015;**3**:18-23

[73] Davenport TH, Ronanki R, et al. Artificial intelligence for the real world. Harvard Business Review. 2018;**96**(1):108-116

[74] Xun X. From cloud computing to cloud manufacturing. Robotics and Computer-Integrated Manufacturing. 2012;**28**(1):75-86

[75] Saberi S, Kouhizadeh M, Sarkis J, Shen L. Blockchain technology and its relationships to sustainable supply chain management. International Journal of Production Research. 2018;**57**:2117-2135

[76] Korpela K, Hallikas J, Dahlberg T. Digital supply chain transformation toward blockchain integration. In: Proceedings of the 50th Hawaii International Conference on System Sciences, Hilton Waikoloa Village, Hawaii, USA. AIS Electronic Library (AISeL); 2017

[77] Lee J, Ni J, Djurdjanovic D, Qiu H, Liao H. Intelligent prognostics tools and e-maintenance. Computers in Industry. 2006;**57**(6):476-489. E-Maintenance Special Issue

[78] Almazrouei SM, Dweiri F, Aydin R, Alnaqbi A. A review on the advancements and challenges of artificial intelligence based models for predictive maintenance of water injection pumps in the oil and gas industry. SN Applied Sciences. 2023;**5**(12):391

Chapter 6

Task Scheduling for Phased Array Multi-Function Radar

Zhen Ding, Petar Przulj, Zhen Qu and Peter Moo

Abstract

Phased array multi-function radar resource management (RRM) is responsible for task scheduling. Finding an optimal solution for task scheduling is an NP-hard problem, so sub-optimal solutions are typically used in real radar systems. In this chapter, we present two existing sub-optimal algorithms: Earliest Start First (EST) and Earliest Deadline (ED). To improve the performance of EST and ED in underloading situations, we propose the Modified EST (MEST) and Modified ED (MED) algorithms. Both EST and ED do not consider task priorities, leading to significant performance degradation. We introduce the Minimum Cost First (MCF) algorithm that replaces the start time first in EST or deadline first in ED. Additionally, we propose an enhanced MCF (EMCF) algorithm to further improve scheduling performance. Simulation results and comparisons demonstrate that MEST and MED perform much better than their unmodified counterparts for loading rates of 80% and below. The MCF algorithm provides a solution that is three times better than EST, while the EMCF algorithm offers a solution that is 6.2 times better than EST. These new algorithms have been evaluated and found to be effective solutions for radar scheduling. The practical implications of these results are significant for real-world radar operations. By incorporating task priorities and improving scheduling efficiency, the proposed algorithms can enhance the overall performance and cost-effectiveness of radar systems. This can lead to more reliable and responsive radar operations, which are crucial for applications such as defense, air traffic control, and weather monitoring.

Keywords: multi-function radar, radar resource management, task scheduling, machine learning, supervised and reinforcement learning, performance evaluation

1. Introduction

Historically, radar systems were designed to perform specific functions using individual mechanical radars. Today, Multi-Function Radars (MFRs) leverage phased arrays to electronically steer the radar beam, enabling rapid execution of multiple functions such as tracking, surveillance, and fire control. To achieve these functions, the start times of individual transmit and receive tasks must be carefully scheduled. Each task is defined by start time t_{start}, duration t_{dwell}, and priority p. A single function may consist of multiple tasks, each with unique t_{start}, t_{dwell}, and p. Efficiently managing these tasks to optimize radar performance is the essence of Radar Resource Management (RRM) [1].

RRM involves selecting, prioritizing, and scheduling tasks. This chapter focuses on the scheduling aspect of RRM. When tasks are initially set for execution, overlaps can occur since radars typically cannot perform tasks simultaneously. Therefore, tasks must be scheduled sequentially. The scheduler's goal is to arrange tasks to avoid overlaps and maximize task completion within specific time intervals, known as execution time windows. Tasks scheduled to start at t_{start} within an execution window are assigned new scheduled times t_{sched} to minimize a predefined cost function. If a task cannot be scheduled within the available time, it is dropped. The scheduler must decide which tasks to drop, usually prioritizing lower-priority tasks to minimize overall cost.

Resource management (RRM) is a critical issue when radar performs multiple functions, each comprising numerous tasks. These tasks request radar resources and have different priorities, often overlapping in time. The radar's ability to assign appropriate resources to all functions and tasks ultimately determines its performance. Scheduling algorithms are designed to sequence tasks to achieve optimal or sub-optimal performance.

Figure 1 illustrates a Navy ship-borne multi-function radar performing volume search, horizon search, target tracking, and missile guidance. Here, RRM is the brain of the radar. It is an essential component; without it, the radar cannot operate. Moreover, an improved RRM scheduler enhances the radar's effectiveness and efficiency.

Optimal task scheduling can theoretically be achieved through brute-force search or branch-and-bound methods, but these approaches are impractical for real-time radar systems due to the NP-hard nature of the scheduling problem [2]. As a result, sub-optimal scheduling algorithms have been developed to approximate the global optimum with greater computational efficiency. Key scheduling algorithms include Earliest Start Time (EST), Earliest Deadline (ED) [3], heuristic-based approaches [4], Random Shifted Start Time (RSST) [5], Gaussian RSST (GRSST) [6], Dual-Side-Scheduling (DSS) [7], task selection (TS) [8], greedy algorithms [9], a thorough literature review of AI-based RRM techniques [10], and a few AI/ML-based methods [11–14].

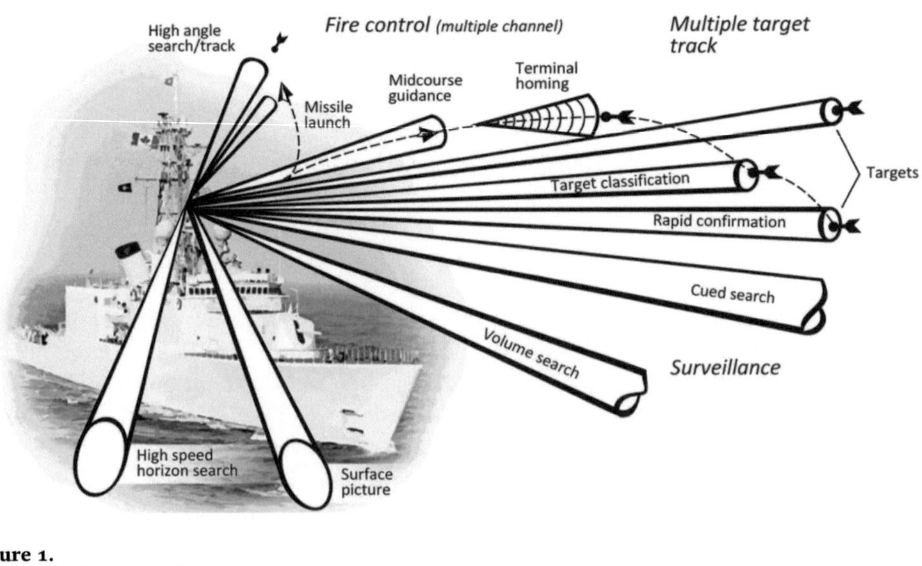

Figure 1.
Navy multi-function radar.

Among these algorithms, RSST and GRSST use random search, which typically find a better solution from more random searches [5, 6]. The DSS algorithm introduces two smaller scheduling windows by a separator [7]. The TS algorithm handles overloading tasks, which will drop less important tasks, resulting in fewer tasks for scheduling [8]. Supervised machine learning and reinforcement learning (RL) are used to improve the efficiency of the Monte Carlo Tree Search (MCTS) [12], which were further enhanced by deep RL (DRL), transfer learning (TL) [13], and a modified MuZero approach [14]. Compared with traditional approaches [2–9], AI/ML methods [11–14] still need better efficiency for real-world applications. Typically, the scheduling time window is around 200 ms. Computation of a practical radar scheduler shall not take too much time from this time window, less than 5%, that is, 10 ms.

We will focus on the traditional scheduling approaches. Among those algorithms, the Earliest Start Time (EST) and Earliest Deadline (ED) algorithms are the simplest and most time efficient. Both algorithms follow a first-come-first-served principle, scheduling tasks based on their start time in EST and their deadline in ED, respectively. This approach involves relocating tasks through a head-to-tail scenario. However, this strategy can result in tasks being scheduled much earlier than necessary, leading to ineffectiveness.

To improve EST's and ED's performance, we propose two new enhancements. First, a modified EST (MEST) is developed, which removes the head-to-tail restriction, resulting in much better performance for underloading situations [15]. We introduced the same modification to ED (MED), achieving similar improvement [16]. Secondly, we noticed that both EST and ED use start time or deadline time for scheduling, but the task priorities have not been used at all. We proposed a priority-based Minimum Cost First (MCF) algorithm and enhanced MCF (EMCF) [17]. Simulation studies show that these two new algorithms perform significantly better than other traditional approaches.

This chapter is organized as follows:

Section 1: Provides a high-level introduction to radar task scheduling, summarizing both traditional and AI/ML approaches.

Section 2: Presents the problem formulation and introduces the cost function.

Section 3: Discusses two baseline algorithms, EST and ED.

Section 4: Describes MEST and MED, along with the simulation results. These modified algorithms address the ineffectiveness of EST and ED in underloading situations.

Section 5: Details both MCF and EMCF, with comparison to the baseline approaches. These new algorithms incorporate priority into the assignment process, significantly reducing costs.

Section 6: Concludes the chapter.

2. Problem formulation

In this section, we formulated radar task scheduling as a cost function optimization problem. Consider a radar system designed to handle N tasks within an execution time window of size L. Each task has six parameters: t_{start}, t_{dwell}, p, $t_{deadline} = t_{start} + t_{dwell}$, $t_{earliest}$, t_{latest}. In this problem, tasks cannot be executed in parallel, so the ideal value for t_{dwell} would be L/N, ensuring that the sum of all tasks' r t_{dwell} equals the entire window size L. These variables are used for all tasks. For a specific task n, we will add *"(n)"* after the variable. For example, $t_{start}(1)$ is the start time for task 1.

The execution window size is normalized such that $L = 1$, with t_{start} ranging from 0 to 1 and t_{dwell} ranging from 0 to $2/N$. In real simulations, the number of tasks in an execution window might be larger or smaller than the designed N tasks. This actual number of tasks is denoted as N_{actual} and the ratio between N_{actual} and N is called the loading rate, $\gamma = N_{actual}/N$. If $\gamma < 100\%$, the radar is under-loaded; if $\gamma > 100\%$, the radar is over-loaded.

For a particular loading rate, the t_{dwell} of all tasks are normalized so that their sum exactly equals the loading rate γ. This process, called t_{dwell} normalization, ensures that loading rates less than or equal to 100% remain underloaded and all tasks fit within the task sequence. Without t_{dwell} normalization, the random distribution of t_{dwell} could cause their sum to exceed 1, necessitating the dropping of a task. This can significantly skew cost results when scheduling for a specific loading rate.

A 5-task sequence with and without t_{dwell} normalization can be seen below:

In **Figure 2**, an unscheduled task sequence is shown where each rounded rectangle represents a task. The left edge of the task indicates its start time, the width corresponds to the dwell time, and the more red and thicker the border, the higher the task's priority. When generating the t_{dwell} for each task, all t_{dwell} values are below average. This results in a task sequence that is supposed to be 100% loaded but only occupies about one-third to one-half of the entire execution window. Conversely, if all t_{dwell} values are above average, the sequence could take much more than 100% of the window. This issue is addressed using t_{dwell} normalization.

Real radar systems have different scheduling time windows, which require a normalized window length for algorithm development, so that performance evaluation can be done fairly. We use time-length "1" as the normalized time window. The normalization process is as follows. Step 1: sum up the dwell times of all tasks. Let's assume the summation time is 0.9 second in total. Step 2: Calculate radar time for the aimed loading rate. For example, 50% loading rate is 0.5 second. Step 3: Recalculate the dwell time for each task, divided by 0.9 and then multiplied by 0.5. The three steps will generate tasks of 50% loading rate, that is, 0.5 seconds of total dwell time.

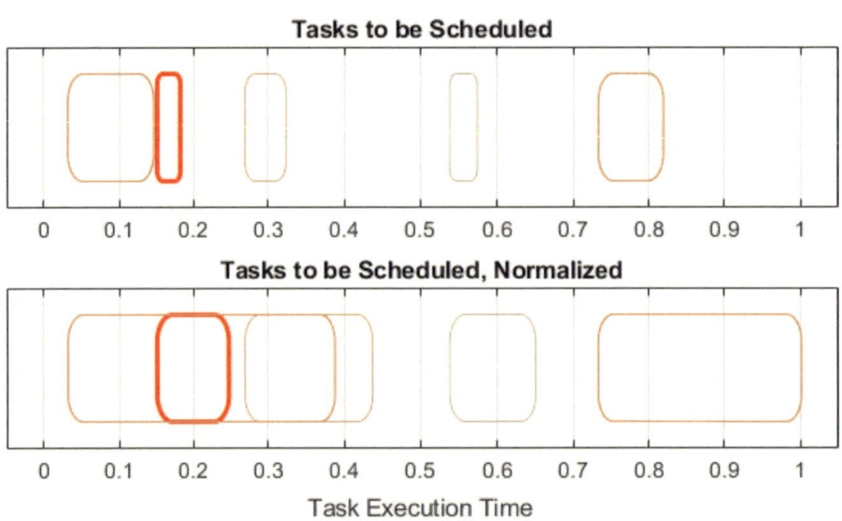

Figure 2.
An unscheduled 100% loaded 5 task sequences without and with t_{dwell} *normalization.*

A scheduling algorithm must arrange the tasks across the execution window such that as many tasks as possible are executed and scheduled as close to their t_{start} as possible. The resulting scheduled time from the algorithm is called t_{sched}. Each task will have an associated cost, $C(n)$, which increases when t_{sched} is far from t_{start}. The total cost, J, of the scheduled times is the sum of the individual costs of the tasks. Relevant cost equations are shown below.

$$t_{sched}(n) = Scheduling\_Algorithm\{t_{start}(n)\} \tag{1}$$

$$C(n) = [p(n) * (t_{sched}(n) - t_{start}(n))]^2 \tag{2}$$

$$J = \frac{1}{N_{actual}} \sum_{n=1}^{N_{actual}} C(n) \tag{3}$$

Each task has a unique identifier number, and each parameter is indexed by this ID. For example, task #2's start time can be written as $t_{start}(2)$. The cost of the task depends on the difference between $t_{sched}(n)$ and $t_{start}(n)$. The farther the scheduled time is from its original start time, the greater the cost accrued. This difference is multiplied by a priority, $p(n)$, implying that the higher the task's priority, the higher the cost of the task. For our purposes, $p(n)$ will be a random number between 0.1 and 0.9 in intervals of 0.1. The difference in time ranges from 0 to 1, and when multiplied by the priority, it will always result in a product lower than 1.

In this report, only underloaded task sequences are evaluated, and we consider the case where all tasks can be scheduled anywhere in the execution window, that is, $t_{earliest}$ = 0 and t_{latest} = 1. Because of this, no tasks need to be dropped, and thus no drop cost is outlined.

3. Two baseline algorithms: The EST and ED

The Earliest Start Time (EST) and Earliest Deadline (ED) algorithms are two baseline scheduling algorithms that are simple to implement and very fast, making them suitable for processing large amounts of tasks in real-world radar systems. However, their performance compared to more advanced methods like machine-learning-based approaches, the branch and bound algorithm, or RSST leaves much to be desired. EST and ED do not consider priority when scheduling; instead, they only consider a task's t_{start} or $t_{deadline}$, respectively.

The EST algorithm schedules tasks in order of increasing start times t_{start}, meaning the task with an earlier start time gets scheduled first. The ED algorithm schedules tasks in order of increasing deadlines $t_{deadline}$, meaning the task with an earlier deadline gets scheduled first. Both algorithms use a head-to-tail connection for scheduling, where the end of one task coincides with the scheduled time of the next task.

One area where EST and ED struggle is in underloaded situations. Due to the head-to-tail restriction, tasks with later start times will be scheduled much earlier. An example of scheduling with both EST and ED for a simple 100% loaded 10-task sequence is shown below in **Figure 3**.

Even though EST and ED schedule tasks quickly, they have two fundamental drawbacks: ineffectiveness in underloading situations and the lack of consideration for task priority in the assignment process.

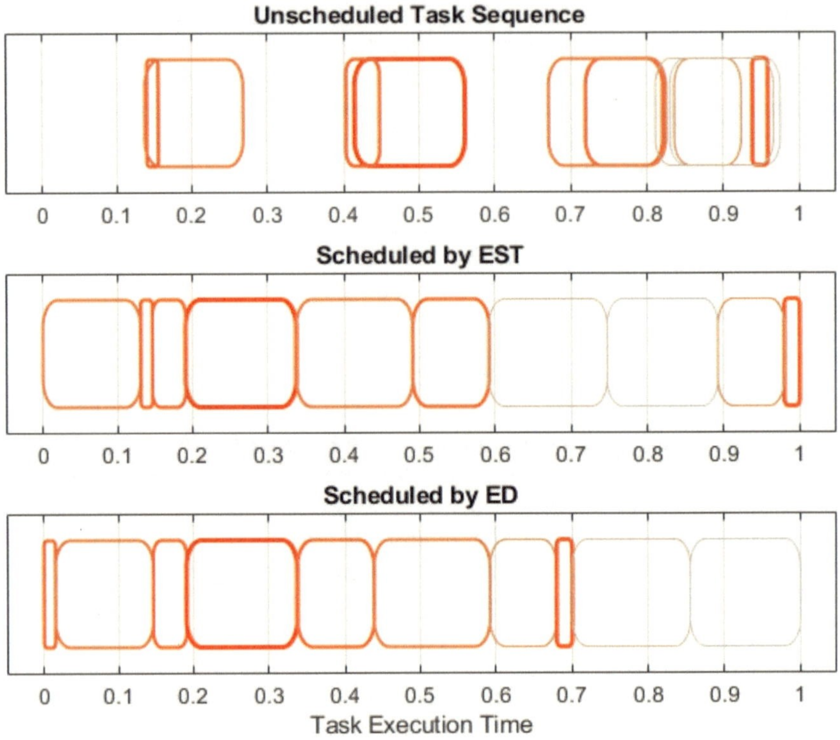

Figure 3.
100% loaded 10 task sequences scheduled with EST and ED.

4. MEST and MED algorithms for underloading situations

In underloading situations, EST and ED tend to arrange tasks toward the left side of the time window, which increases the overall cost. To overcome this drawback, we proposed the Modified Earliest Start Time (MEST) and Modified Earliest Deadline (MED) algorithms. These enhanced versions of the baseline EST and ED algorithms maintain similar speed and the ability to handle large amounts of tasks. Like their unmodified counterparts, the modified algorithms schedule tasks in the same order. However, the restriction of scheduling tasks head-to-tail is relaxed.

For the next task with the earliest t_{start} or $t_{deadline}$ among the unscheduled tasks, the modified algorithm schedules the task at its t_{start} provided that the sum of the remaining tasks' t_{dwell} does not exceed the remaining time in the window. Otherwise, MEST/MED schedules it right after the previous task (head-to-tail connection). MEST and MED aim to improve the performance of EST and ED in underloaded cases by scheduling tasks right at their t_{start} whenever possible.

In overloaded situations, the modified algorithms will perform similar to EST and ED since the modified versions would only perform head-to-tail connections (with no remaining time). Because of this, the MEST and MED algorithms are almost always better than the EST and ED algorithms across all loading rates. An example of an underloaded task sequence scheduled using ED and MED is shown below.

As seen in **Figure 4**, later tasks such as the one starting at around 0.9 need to be scheduled much earlier when using a head-to-tail connection as seen when scheduling by ED. MED resolves this by scheduling it instead at its original t_{start}.

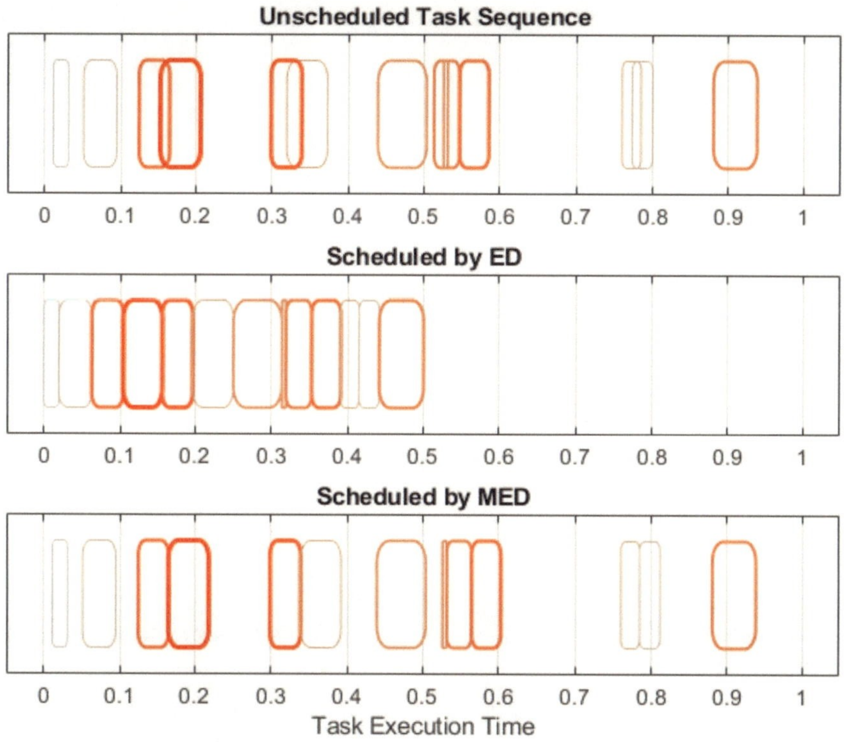

Figure 4.
50% loaded 25 task sequences scheduled by ED and MED.

The MEST and MED algorithms improve the baseline algorithms in underloaded cases by removing the head-to-tail restriction inherent in both. By eliminating this restriction, the modified algorithms perform much better than their unmodified counterparts for loading rates of 80% and below. For all other underloaded loading rates, the modified algorithms accrue costs very similar to their respective unmodified algorithms. The time efficiency of MEST and MED is comparable to EST and ED, making them very feasible for real-world radar systems. This "modified" approach could be applied to other scheduling algorithms to increase their efficacy in underloaded circumstances if a similar head-to-tail restriction exists.

The algorithms are compared by running 10,000 simulations with randomly generated tasks for 13 different loading rates. The simulated multi-function radar is designed to handle 50 tasks within the execution window (N = 50). The average cost for both algorithms is calculated using eqs. (1) through (3). The average computation time used for each algorithm and loading rate is recorded from MATLAB. Since modified versions would have the same performance as the unmodified algorithms for overloaded cases, only loading rates under 100% were considered. The following loading rates were used: 10, 20, 30, 40, 50, 60, 70, 80, 90, 92, 94, 96, 98%. The differences between EST and MEST are largely the same as the differences between ED and MED. To simplify the report results, ED will be used to represent the unmodified algorithms and MED will be used to represent the modified algorithms.

Each task has a t_{start} generated using a uniform distribution between 0 and $1 - t_{dwell}$ such that all tasks cannot extend past the end of the execution window. The t_{dwell} is generated using a uniform distribution between 0 and $\frac{2}{N}$ with an average of $\frac{1}{N}$ and thus

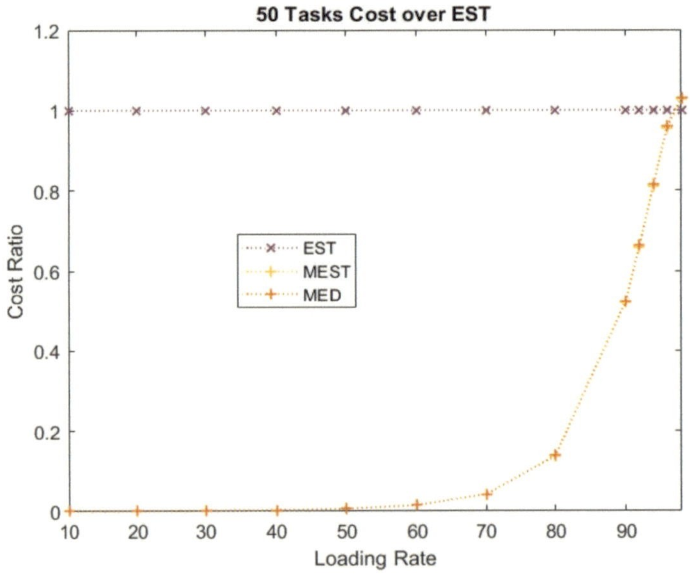

Figure 5.
Cost ratio of 50 task long task sequences scheduled by EST, MEST, and MED over EST over different loading rates. Note that EST and ED have similar cost ratio.

on average sum to 1. The $t_{earliest}$ and the t_{latest} are set to 0 and 1 respectively meaning all tasks can be scheduled anywhere within the window. The p of each task is generated uniformly between 0.1 and 0.9 in increments of 0.1. For each loading rate, γ, the number of tasks to be scheduled, N_{actual}, is given by $N_{actual} = \gamma * N$.

Figure 5 illustrates the performance improvement, showing that a lower loading rate results in better improvement. **Figure 6** demonstrates that the computation time is less than 0.1 ms, making it highly efficient for practical applications.

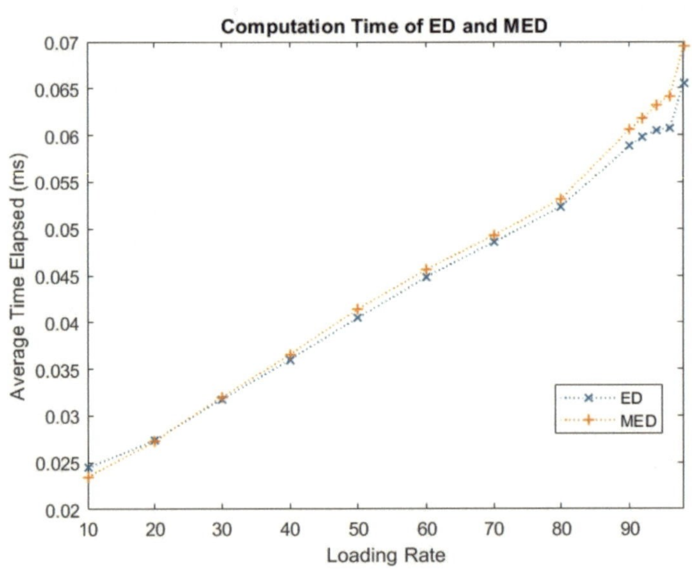

Figure 6.
Average times of 50 task sequences scheduled by ED and MED over different loading rates.

5. MCF and EMCF algorithms with priority-embedded

These four algorithms (EST, ED, MEST, and MED) missed a critical factor: task prioritization. Higher priority tasks should be treated differently in scheduling algorithms, as they directly affect the cost to be optimized. We propose the Minimum Cost First (MCF) algorithm, which incorporates priority when assigning tasks. Furthermore, an enhanced version of MCF is also proposed.

5.1 MCF algorithm

The MCF algorithm aims to minimize the total scheduled task sequence cost through a greedy approach. The algorithm calculates the cost of each task when hypothetically scheduling it and then schedules the task with the lowest cost. Instead of only scheduling on one side of the execution window, tasks are scheduled by alternating from the start and the end of the window. This reduces the chance of tasks being left behind, as tasks not scheduled near their start time will incur higher costs as more tasks get scheduled.

Alternating the tasks also lowers the cost if tasks are left behind, as these tasks will be scheduled near the middle of the window where they would usually be scheduled at the end if not alternated. The pseudo-code of the MCF algorithm is shown in **Table 1**. The MCF algorithm is put through numerical simulations to find its average cost and time. **Figures 7** and **8** show the average costs and cost ratio over EST using the classic cost function. **Figures 9** and **10** show the same but using the tauless cost function. The computation time of MCF is shown in **Figure 11**. In these figures, blue, red, and yellow represent EST, RSST, and MCF, respectively.

Initialize variables: wind_start = 0, wind_end = 1, bool_start = true
For i = 1:N
If bool_start // Schedule at start of sequence
costs_start ← calculate cost of all tasks using Eq. 2–5 if scheduled at wind_start
min_cost, min_idx ← find minimum cost from costs_start
t_{sched}*(min_idx) = wind_start, bool_start = false*
wind_start = wind_start + t_{dwell}*(min_idx)*
Else // Scheduling at end of sequence
costs_end ← calculate cost of all tasks using if scheduled at wind_end - t_{dwell}
min_cost, min_idx ← find minimum cost from costs_end
wind_end = wind_end - t_{dwell}*(min_idx)*
t_{sched}*(min_idx) = wind_end, bool_start = true*
End
costs(min_idx) = min_cost
p(min_idx) = Inf // Already scheduled tasks produce an infinite cost
End

Table 1.
MCF scheduling algorithm.

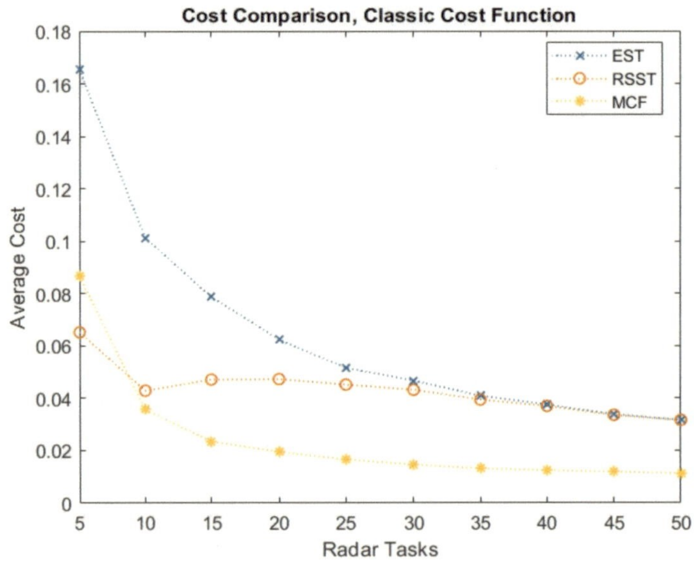

Figure 7.
Average cost of MCF (yellow) compared with other algorithms using the classic cost function.

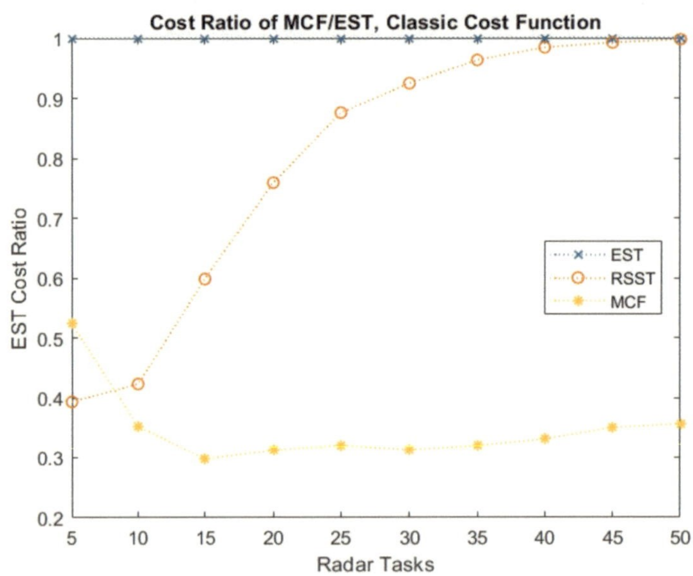

Figure 8.
Cost ratio of MCF/EST compared with ratios of other algorithms using the classic cost function.

As seen in **Figures** 7 and **8**, when using the classic cost function, MCF has much lower costs than both EST and RSST. Its average cost goes as low as 0.3 times that of EST and averages around 0.42 times over all tasks. RSST still outperforms MCF with five tasks, as RSST almost always gets the optimal solution with small numbers of tasks and a large enough K iterations.

Figures 9 and **10** illustrate how the change in cost function can drastically affect the cost of MCF. When using the tauless cost function, MCF's cost is significantly higher than EST, reaching up to 5 times larger than EST and averaging 3.3 times larger

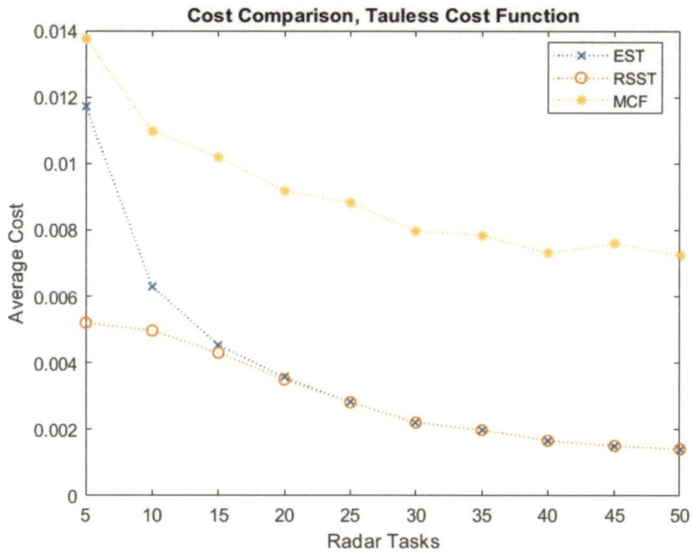

Figure 9.
Average cost of MCF compared with other algorithms using the tauless cost function.

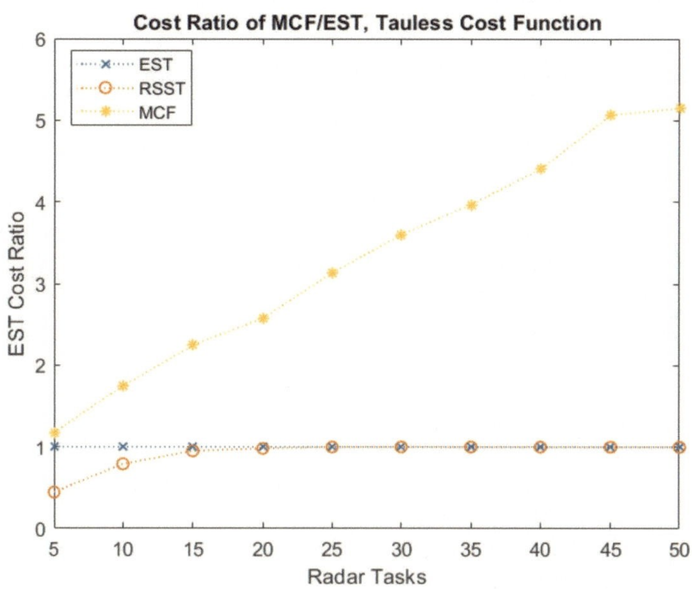

Figure 10.
Cost ratio of MCF/EST compared with ratios of other algorithms using the tauless cost function.

over all tasks. This sudden change in cost between cost functions occurs due to how MCF schedules tasks and how the classic cost function operates when scheduling at the ends of the execution window.

When scheduling at the start or end of the execution window, the classic cost function only depends on the priority of the task, regardless of its position in the window. For subsequent tasks, the distance between t_{start} and t_{sched} becomes more significant as tasks are scheduled further from the ends of the window. This results in

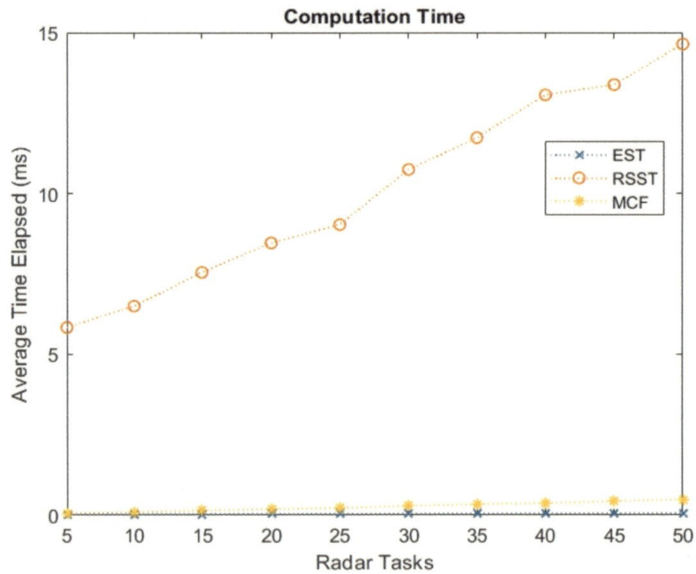

Figure 11.
Computation time of MCF compared with other algorithms.

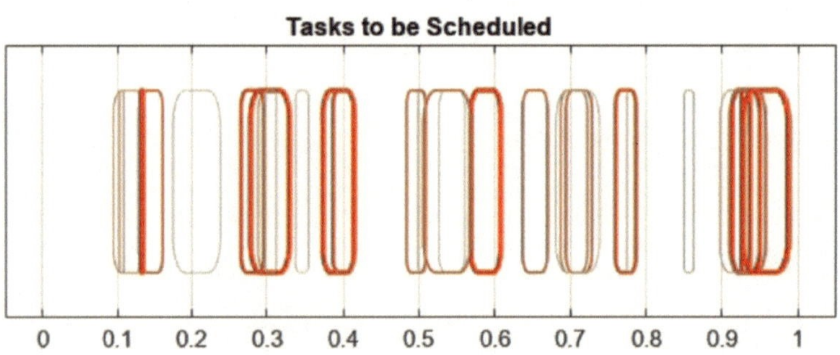

Figure 12.
Example task sequence to be scheduled using MCF.

an unintuitive optimal scheduling pattern and those algorithms like EST generally do not perform well in, but MCF matches very well.

When using the tauless cost function, scheduling becomes more intuitive. Scheduling the task with the minimum cost first often results in low-priority tasks being scheduled first, which might cause high-priority tasks to be scheduled later, thus significantly increasing the cost. Missing one high-priority task to be scheduled before a lower-priority task can cause the high-priority task to accrue massive costs until it is the last task and needs to be scheduled.

Figure 11 shows the average computation time of MCF. MCF averages 0.47 ms over all tasks and is very comparable to the runtime of EST. MCF improves on the cost of EST and RSST, when using the classic cost function, while also being close to the computation time of EST. A drawback of MCF is that even with alternating, tasks are still left behind and are scheduled much later than they should be. An example of this phenomenon can be seen in **Figures 12** and **13**.

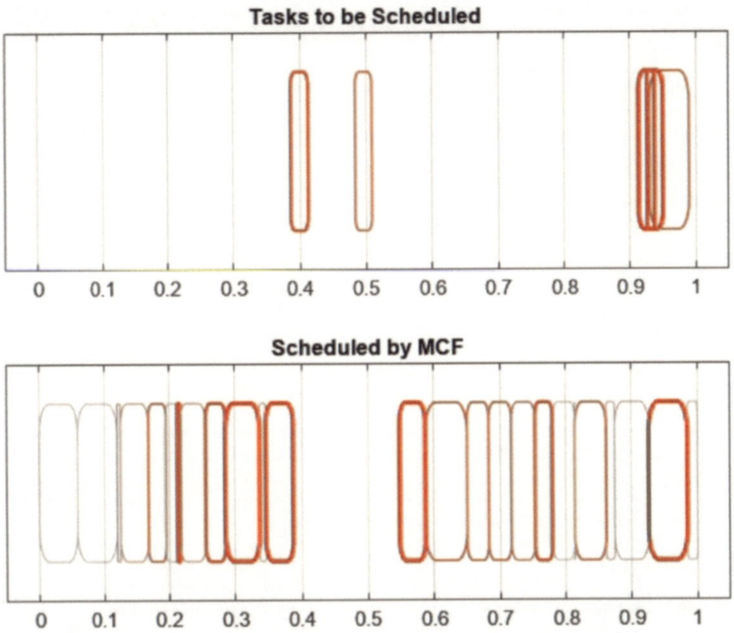

Figure 13.
MCF scheduling algorithm near completion.

In **Figure 10**, tasks that are between 0.9 and 1 in the execution window are left behind and will only get scheduled after every other task is scheduled. An enhanced version of the algorithm addresses this issue and decreases the cost by scheduling based on the overall cost instead of just the per-task cost.

5.2 EMCF algorithm

The Enhanced Minimum Cost First EMCF algorithm improves the cost performance of MCF at the expense of time efficiency. EMCF schedules tasks based on the total scheduled task sequence cost Eq. (1) instead of the per-task cost Eq. (2). Like MCF, tasks are scheduled by alternating between the start and end of the execution window. To choose which task to schedule, three tasks are selected: one with the earliest start time EST, one with the earliest deadline ED, and one with the minimum cost MCF. When scheduling at the end, the latest start time or deadline is chosen instead of the earliest.

Only three tasks are chosen to reduce computation time while maintaining a lower cost. For each task, the remaining sequence is completed using a simple scheduling algorithm like EST. The task that gets scheduled is the one that results in the lowest overall cost of the three. The pseudo-code of the EMCF algorithm is shown in **Table 2**.

When running the EST algorithm in lines 5–9 and 12–16, t_{shift} is used to alter the starting times such that some tasks always start first and others start last while keeping t_{start} the same for cost calculation purposes. By making t_{shift} equal to times that are before and after the execution window, tasks can be forced to get scheduled at the start or end without interfering with the rest of the scheduling. Numerical simulations are performed, the cost graphs are seen in **Figures 14–18** shows the time graph.

Initialize variables: wind_start = 0, wind_end = 1, bool_start = true, $t_{deadline}=t_{start}+t_{dwell}$, $t_{shift}=t_{start}$
For i = 1:N
If bool_start
$(idx_{EST}, idx_{ED}, idx_{MCF}) \leftarrow$ *find indices of unscheduled tasks with earliest* t_{start}, $t_{deadline}$ *and minimum cost at wind_start.*
$costs_{EST} \leftarrow$ *conduct EST Scheduling Algorithm using* t_{shift}.
$prev\_t_{shift} = t_{shift}$
$costs_{ED} \leftarrow$ *conduct EST Scheduling Algorithm using* $t_{shift}(idx_{ED}) = -N + i-1$.
$t_{shift} = prev\_t_{shift}$
$costs_{MCF} \leftarrow$ *conduct EST Scheduling Algorithm using* $t_{shift}(idx_{MCF}) = -N + i-1$.
Else
$(idx_{EST}, idx_{ED}, idx_{MCF}) \leftarrow$ *find indices of unscheduled tasks with latest* t_{start}, $t_{deadline}$ *and minimum cost at wind_end.*
$costs_{EST} \leftarrow$ *conduct EST Scheduling Algorithm using* t_{shift}.
$prev\_t_{shift} = t_{shift}$
$costs_{ED} \leftarrow$ *conduct EST Scheduling Algorithm using* $t_{shift}(idx_{ED}) = N-i + 1$.
$t_{shift} = prev\_t_{shift}$
$cost_{MCF} \leftarrow$ *conduct EST Scheduling Algorithm using* $t_{shift}(idx_{MCF}) = N-i + 1$.
End
$t_{shift} = prev\_t_{shift}$
$costs_{min} \leftarrow$ *find minimum of: sum of* $costs_{EST}$, *sum of* $costs_{ED}$ *and sum of* $costs_{MCF}$.
$idx \leftarrow$ *pick the task that corresponds to* $costs_{min}$.
$costs(idx) = costs_{min}(idx)$
If bool_start: $t_{shift}(idx) = -N + i-1$
If not bool_start: $t_{shift}(idx) = N-i + 1$
bool_start = not bool_start
update wind_start and wind_end using task idx.
End

Table 2.
EMCF scheduling algorithm.

With the classic cost function, EMCF improves upon MCF in terms of cost for all numbers of tasks. From **Figures 14** and **15**, the EMCF algorithm produces a cost that goes as low as 0.11x of EST and averages around 0.19x of EST over all tasks. EMCF is strictly better than MCF in terms of cost for every number of tasks. EMCF has a slightly higher cost than RSST at five tasks as RSST usually gets the optimal solution with enough iterations at low numbers of tasks. Note that the absolute cost values are indicators how the algorithms perform, but the cost ratios provide a better comparison to the baseline algorithm. Here, the EST algorithm is chosen as the baseline for the cost ratio calculation.

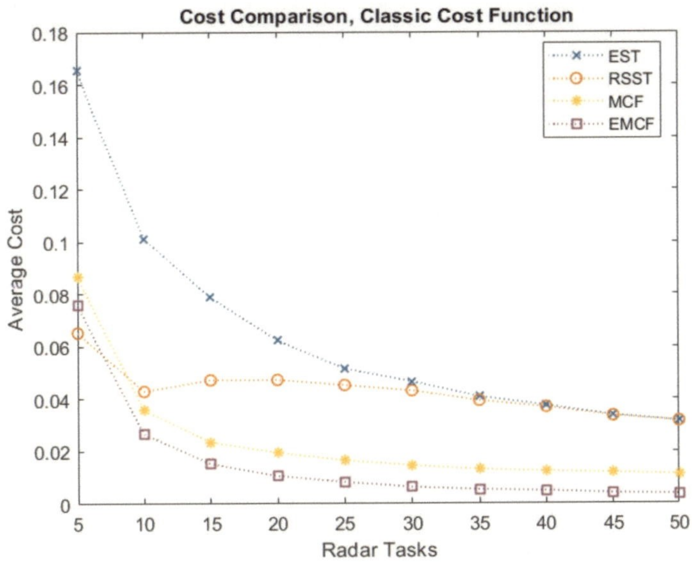

Figure 14.
Average cost of EMCF (purple) compared with other algorithms using the classic cost function.

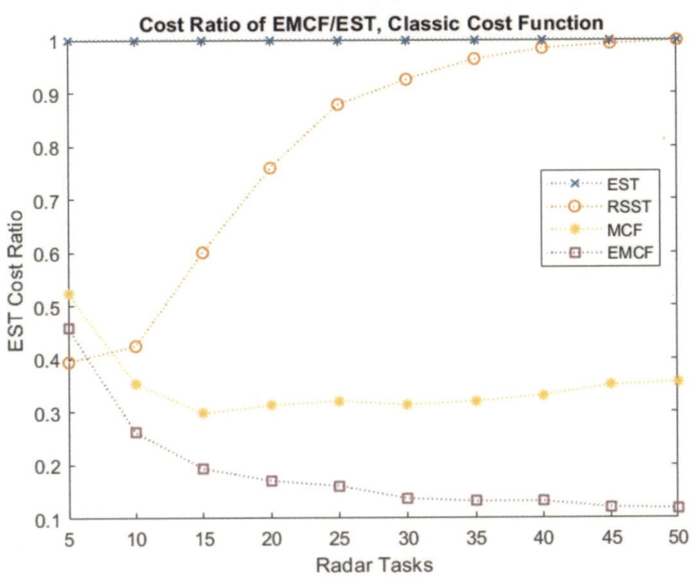

Figure 15.
Cost ratio of EMCF/EST compared with ratios of other algorithms using the classic cost function.

In the figures below, blue, red, yellow, and pink represent EST, RSST, MCF, and EMCF, respectively.

Using the tauless cost function, EMCF drastically improves upon the MCF algorithm. By checking how scheduling a task affects the entire sequence, the algorithm can make sure that scheduling a task does not push back higher priority tasks later. Because of this, EMCF is suitable to schedule using the tauless cost function and produces less costs than EST and RSST. EMCF accrues costs around 0.5x of EST.

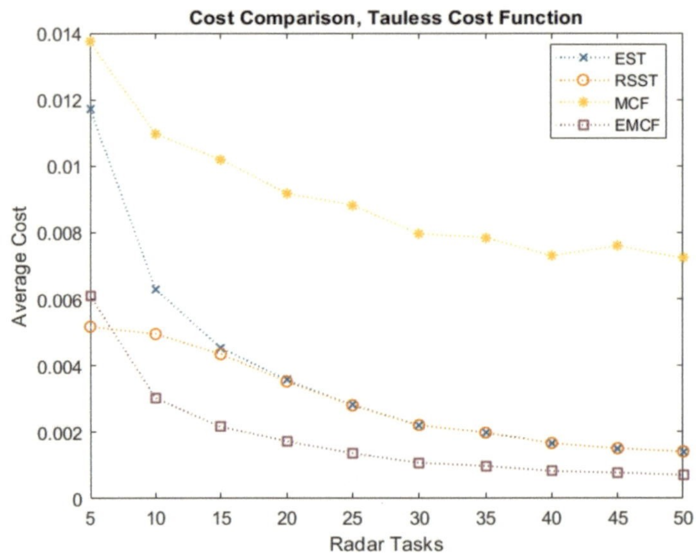

Figure 16.
Average cost of EMCF compared with other algorithms using the tauless cost function.

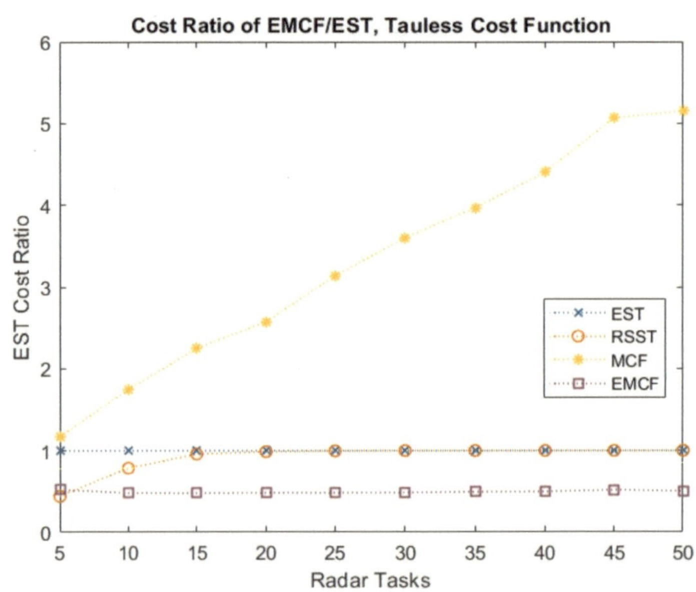

Figure 17.
Cost ratio of EMCF/EST compared with ratios of other algorithms using the tauless cost function.

The EMCF algorithm performs better than all other algorithms in terms of cost using both classic and tauless cost functions. However, the time it takes to run is larger than EST and MCF but is still less than RSST. EMCF takes around 4.7 ms on average over all number of tasks. If the radar system allows for the increased computation time, it is recommended to use EMCF over MCF.

The number of times that each sub-algorithm in EMCF leads to the scheduled task is analyzed. The EMCF algorithm and which task is selected to get scheduled is

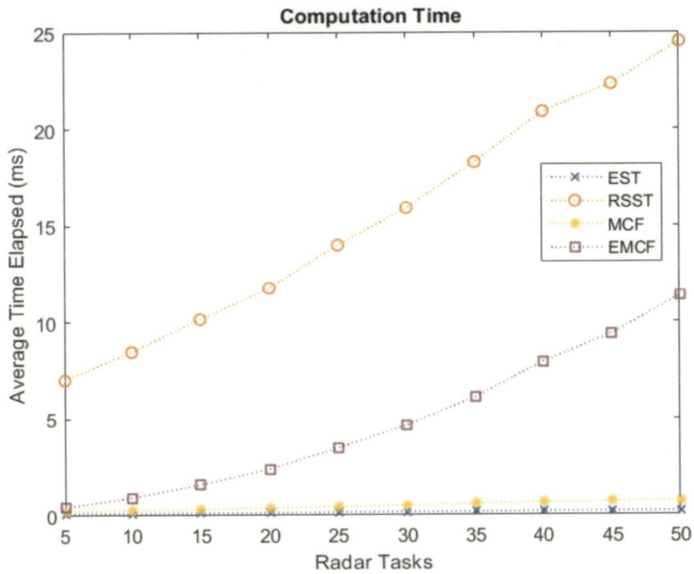

Figure 18.
Computation time of EMCF compared with MCF and other algorithms.

Algorithms	Number of tasks									
	5	*10*	*15*	*20*	*25*	*30*	*35*	*40*	*45*	*50*
EST	3	3	3	4	4	5	4	5	5	5
ED	3	3	4	4	4	4	5	4	4	5
MCF	25	25	25	25	24	24	24	24	24	23
EST & ED	10	14	17	18	20	22	23	24	25	26
EST & MCF	5	5	5	5	5	4	4	4	4	4
ED & MCF	5	5	4	4	4	4	4	4	3	3
EST & ED & MCF	49	45	42	40	39	37	36	35	35	34

Table 3.
Percentages of combined best tasks.

somewhat independent of which cost function you use. Because of this, only the results from using the classic cost function are used. **Table 3** shows the percentages of how often each algorithm or group of algorithms provide the best task with the lowest total cost. **Table 4** shows the percentages of how often the individual algorithms provide the best task.

The computation time of EMCF is well below 5% of the time widow 200 ms when there are 45 or less tasks. Note that the number of tasks in a real radar system is 20–30. The EMCF algorithm maximizes the performance and keeps the computation practical.

For most cases, choosing a task with EST, ED, or MCF provides the same solution and is thus used as the “best” solution. From **Table 1**, MCF provides the most unique

Algorithms	Number of tasks									
	5	*10*	*15*	*20*	*25*	*30*	*35*	*40*	*45*	*50*
EST	31	31	32	32	33	33	33	34	34	34
ED	31	31	32	32	32	33	33	33	33	34
MCF	39	37	36	36	35	34	33	33	33	32

Table 4.
Percentages of single best task.

best solutions out of the three algorithms as EST and ED are likely to be the same task. **Table 2** shows us that for smaller numbers of tasks, MCF provides the best task while with larger numbers of tasks, EST, ED, and MCF all provide the best task out of the three at the same rate.

6. Conclusion

Two modified approaches to baseline radar task scheduling algorithms were proposed: Modified Earliest Start Time (MEST) and Modified Earliest Deadline (MED). These algorithms improve upon the unmodified versions in underloaded cases by removing the head-to-tail restriction inherent in both. By eliminating this restriction, the modified algorithms perform much better than their unmodified counterparts for loading rates of 80% and below. Additionally, two algorithms were proposed using the cost function as a scheduling tool. The first algorithm, Minimum Cost First (MCF), schedules tasks based on the lowest individual task cost. The second algorithm, Enhanced Minimum Cost First (EMCF), schedules tasks based on overall task cost. The MCF algorithm provides a solution that is three times better than EST, while the EMCF algorithm offers a solution that is 6.2 times better than EST. The proposed scheduling algorithms are suitable for real-world radar systems due to their low computation time and low costs.

For future work, efficiency improvements are needed for current AI/ML approaches. Combining AI/ML with traditional methods may offer new solutions for radar scheduling. Efficiency could be directly enhanced through parallel and/or quantum computing.

Author details

Zhen Ding*, Petar Przulj, Zhen Qu and Peter Moo
Radar Sensing and Exploitation Section, Defence R&D Canada – Ottawa Research Centre, Canada

*Address all correspondence to: zhen.ding@drdc-rddc.gc.ca

References

[1] Moo P, Ding Z. Adaptive Radar Resource Management. Cambridge, Massachusetts, USA: Academic Press; 2015

[2] Lenstra J, Brucker P. Complexity of machine scheduling problems. Annals of Discrete Mathematics. 1977;**1**:343-362

[3] Bratley P, Florian M, Robillard P. Scheduling with earliest start and due date constraints. Naval Research Logistics Quarterly. 1971;**18**(4):511-519

[4] Mir H, Abdelaziz F. A heuristic task scheduling method for multifunction radar. Journal of Telecommunication, Electronic and Computer Engineering. 2017;**9**(7):89-92

[5] Qu Z, Ding Z, Moo P. A radar task scheduling method using random shifted start time with the EST algorithm. In: IEEE Radar Conference. 2019. pp. 1-5

[6] Ding Z, Przulj P, Qu Z, Moo P. Radar task scheduling with Gaussian random shifted start time. In: IEEE Radar Conference. Denver, Colorado, USA: IEEE; 2024. pp. 1-5

[7] Qu Z, Ding Z, Moo P. Dual-side scheduling for radar resource management. In: 2020 21st International Radar Symposium (IRS). Radar Symposium (IRS). Boston, Massachusetts, USA: IEEE; pp. 260-263

[8] Qu Z, Ding Z, Moo P. Reinforcement learning based task selection and scheduling for radar resource management. In: DRDC Scientific Report, Defence Research and Development Canada (DRDC): Ottawa, ON, Canada. DRDC-RDDC-2023-R039. 2023. pp. 1-34

[9] Huang L, Zhang Y, Li Q, Pan C, Song J. Task-scheduling scheme based on greedy algorithm in integrated radar and communication systems. The IET Journal of Engineering. 2019;**2019**(19):1-6

[10] Shaghaghi M, Adve R, Ding Z. Multi-function cognitive radar task scheduling using Monte Carlo tree search and policy networks. IET Radar, Sonar, Navigation. 2018;**12**(12):1437-1447

[11] Hashmi U, Akba S, Adve R, Moo P, Ding Z. Artificial intelligence meets radar resource management: A comprehensive background and literature review. IET Radar, Sonar and Navigation. 2023;**17**(2):1234-1254

[12] Akbar S, Adve R, Ding Z, Moo P. Transfer-based DRL for task scheduling in dynamic environments for cognitive radar. IEEE Transactions on Aerospace and Electronic Systems. 2024; **60**(1):37-50

[13] Gaafar M, Shaghaghi M, Adve R, Ding Z. Reinforcement learning for cognitive radar task scheduling. In: IEEE Radar Conference. Oklahoma City, Oklahoma, USA: IEEE; 2018

[14] Akbar S, Adve R, Ding Z, Moo P. Task scheduling in cognitive multifunction radar using model-based DRL. IEEE Transactions on Aerospace and Electronic Systems. 2024;**60**(1): 37-50

[15] Ding Z, Qu Z, Moo P. A modified earliest start time (MEST) algorithm for multi-function radar task scheduling. In: 2022 23rd International Radar Symposium (IRS). Gdańsk, Poland: IEEE; 2022. p. 323-326

[16] Ding Z, Przulj P, Qu Z, Moo P. Development of modified earliest start time and modified earliest deadline algorithms - A radar task scheduling modification for underloaded scenarios.

In: DRDC Scientific Report, Defence Research and Development Canada (DRDC): Ottawa, ON, Canada. DRDC-RDDC-2024-R141. 2024. pp. 1-23

[17] Ding Z, Przulj P, Qu Z, Moo P. Minimum cost first radar scheduling algorithms based on individual task and sequence costs. In: DRDC Scientific Report, Defence Research and Development Canada (DRDC): Ottawa, ON, Canada. DRDC-RDDC-2024-R157. 2024. pp. 1-25

Chapter 7

Task Allocation Techniques for Real-Time Mixed Criticality Multicore Systems: A Survey

Cristina-Sorina Stângaciu

Abstract

With the development of the Internet of Things and distributed systems, both the applications and the hardware support increased their complexity. This evolution resulted in an inevitable move toward multicore platforms at the edge of the Internet of Things in real-time and safety-critical systems. This shift to multicore architectures reflects also in the transformation and evolution of the mixed-criticality real-time task scheduling techniques, which still face several challenges due to their restricted resources and safety-critical aspects that include determinism, predictability, task isolation, resource management and low power consumption. The goal of this chapter is to present a survey on the state of the art multicore scheduling techniques, with a focus on task-allocation algorithms for mixed-criticality real-time systems, while identifying the research gaps and future trends.

Keywords: real-time, mixed-criticality systems, task scheduling, multicore processors, partitioning

1. Introduction

In the context of the continuous development of the Internet of Things (IoT) together with other types of distributed systems, the applications running on these systems become more and more complex in order to satisfy the increasing demands of communication, connectivity, varied functionalities and fast responsiveness. These demands regarding functionality and performance, coming from the applications side, are pushing forward the evolution of the hardware architectures that support them [1, 2].

The complexity of the applications running at the edge of IoT or in other distributed embedded systems having a direct interaction with the environment, such as cyber-physical systems, often imply both real-time and non-real time, critical and non-critical interactions between these systems and the environment in which they run [3]. This complex interaction led to conflicting requirements related to the complexity of the applications, on one hand, and related to resource constraints imposed by the end devices at the edge of IoT or by other embedded systems, on the other hand. In order to deal with safety assurance and real-time functionalities, while reconciling these conflicting requirements in the context of real-time and safety-criticality systems, a new type of system was defined, named the mixed-criticality systems (MCS). This concept defines systems with two or more criticality-level components running on the same hardware. Their goal is to reconcile the need of partitioning for safety assurance while still efficiently sharing resources [4].

MCS were initially developed in the context of automotive, [5] being the first paper to formalize them. Since then, they were adopted in different fields, such as cyber-physical systems [3], Industry 4.0 [6], avionics [7], and the Industrial Internet of Things [8].

2. Organization

This chapter continues with the following sections: Section 3 presents the background and theoretical aspects regarding real-time systems in general, while Section 4 focuses on mixed-criticality systems, task modeling, execution behavior and scheduling in multicore systems with a focus on task allocation. A methodology for mixed-criticality task scheduling is proposed in Section 5 and the open issues are presented in Section 6. This chapter ends by presenting the main conclusions in Section 7.

3. Background

The need to guarantee real-time services in critical environment led to the initial proposal and formalization of the real-time systems (RTS) paradigm by Liu and Layland in 1973 [9]. Real-time systems are defined as those systems for which not only the correctness of the provided results is important, but also the time at which these results are generated. Thus, special efforts have been made toward the development of mathematical models, and scheduling methods in order to guarantee that all the time constraints are respected.

According to the strictness of their time constraints (i.e., deadlines), the real-time systems are classified into [10, 11]:

1. Hard RTS – in this class of systems, missing a deadline leads to a total system failure (e.g., airbag system).

2. Firm RTS – infrequent deadline misses are tolerable, but the usefulness of the result is zero after its deadline (e.g., traffic management).

3. Soft RTS – the usefulness of a result degrades after its deadline, leading to a quality of service degradation (e.g., audio/video streaming).

A similar classification into hard, firm and soft extends to the software running on these systems and includes the so-called tasks, which represent basic units of execution for each application running in a real-time system.

The classical real-time task models contain specifications about the time constraints of the tasks. Based on their arrival pattern, tasks can be periodic, sporadic or aperiodic.

Periodic tasks are activated and executed within regular time intervals called period. They are characterized by their execution time C in the form of Worst Case

Execution Time (WCET), period T and relative deadline D, which can be equal to the period if we consider implicit deadlines [9]. Each task must execute once and only once in the interval between its activation time and its deadline. According to Liu and Layland's model proposed in Ref. [9], for a task τ_i, we have the following specifications:

$$\tau_i = \{C_i; T_i; D_i\} \tag{1}$$

where C_i represents the computation time, T_i the period and D_i the deadline for the task τ_i.

If the activation of a certain task is done with an offset, relative to the system's activation time, a new parameter called phase (ϕ) is added [10–12]:

$$\tau_i = \{\phi_i; C_i; T_i; D_i\} \tag{2}$$

For task with no offset and implicit deadlines, the model could be simplified to the following equation [9–12]:

$$\tau_i = \{C_i; T_i\} \tag{3}$$

From these parameters, others can be determined, such as the processor utilization factor [9–12]:

$$U_i = C_i/T_i \tag{4}$$

Eq. (4), in fact, represents the definition of the processor utilization of a task.

Sporadic tasks are activated at arbitrary points in time, but with defined inter-arrival times between two consecutive invocations. They are characterized by their execution time C in the form of Worst Case Execution Time (WCET), minimum inter-arrival time T and relative deadline D [13]. For a task τ_i, we have, the same parameters as in Eqs. (1), (2) or (3), but with a different meaning for T.

Aperiodic tasks are activated at any point in time but only once. They are characterized by their execution time C in the form of Worst Case Execution Time (WCET), arrival time A and relative deadline D. For a task τ_i, we have:

$$\tau_i = \{C_i; A_i; D_i\} \tag{5}$$

Each instance of a task is called job. In classical real-time systems, usually a job inherits the parameters of the task it represents, but it can also be represented using specific parameters, like in eq. (6) for a job j of task i:

$$\tau_{ij} = \{C_{ij}; A_{ij}; d_{ij}\} \tag{6}$$

where d_{ij} represents the absolute deadline, equal to $A_{ij} + D_i$. For a periodic task, with no offset for its activation, $A_{ij} = (j-1) * T_i$.

An example of a task set execution on a single processor, simulated in SimSo [14], can be seen in **Figure 1**. The task set consists of four tasks: $T1$ and $T2$ periodic, $T3$ sporadic, with an offset of 10, and $T4$ aperiodic, with the parameters represented in eq. (7), according to Eq. (1) for $T1$-$T2$, Eq. (2) for $T3$, and Eq. (5) for $T4$:

$$T1 = \{3; 10; 10\}; T2 = \{4; 15; 15\}; T3 = \{10; 3; 20; 20\}; T4 = \{2; 13; 25\}; \tag{7}$$

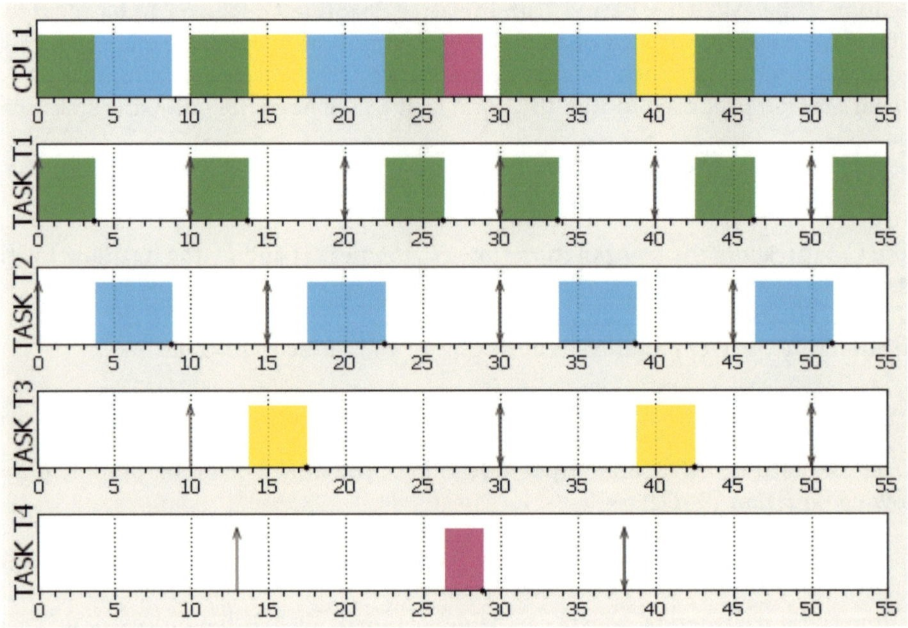

Figure 1.
Example of uniprocessor real-time task set execution.

In this figure, the up arrows represent the activation times and the down arrows the deadlines.

Since their first introduction into the literature, real-time systems, together with their programming and scheduling models, have become increasingly prevalent in critical fields such as chemical factories, nuclear facilities, space exploration or military applications [1], and in the relatively recent years these systems' integration extended to fields like IoT, automated driving or healthcare [15].

4. Mixed-criticality real-time systems

Mixed-criticality systems are basically a type of real-time system where tasks are valued by their criticality by classifying them into distinct levels of assurance against failure, such as mission-critical and safety-critical [1, 4].

4.1 Task models and execution behavior

The classical real-time task model only specifies the temporal behavior of a job and does not express its criticality, so new parameters were introduced. The first mixed-criticality task model is considered the one proposed in 2007 by Vestal [5]. It represents a generalization of the sporadic task model introduces by Mok in 1983 [13]. Vestal's model is characterized by four parameters: criticality level L_i which range from A to E (A being associated with catastrophic and E with no effect), period T_i, deadline D_i and computation time C_i represented as a vector of WCETs, one for each criticality level, usually ranging from the most optimistic value for the lowest criticality level to the most pessimistic value for the highest one. Thus, the model from Eq. (1), according to Vestal's model [5], becomes:

$$\tau_i = \{L_i; C_i = \{C_{i1}; C_{i2} \dots C_{iN}\}; T_i; D_i\} \tag{8}$$

where L_i is the criticality level of task τ_i, and C_i is a vector of N values, where N is equal to the order of the criticality level L_i. Thus, a task of the lowest criticality level will have only a value in the C_i vector, corresponding to its own criticality, a task of a second criticality level (considered from low to high), will have two values and so on.

After Vestal's task model, other generic models were proposed in the literature, where other parameters are also vectors of values depending on criticality level. Following the model proposed by Vestal, new models were developed. In MCS, the software execution is also modeled at job level. Some of the most popular proposed models and their characteristics are presented briefly in **Table 1** from Appendix A, where the criticality level, execution time, period and deadline are the same with the ones expressed by Eq. (8), even if the notations are sometimes different as we can see in the case of the criticality level expressed by L, l, χ, ζ or k in the period expressed by T or p.

The majority of mixed-criticality models were created in an incremental manner based on the structure proposed by Vestal as a generic model [5]. The models started from the main four parameters: L—criticality level, T—period, D—deadline, C—computation time and then were extended by adding parameters or by changing some of the existing ones [15]. For example, some models include the activation time or release time with the same meaning as the one expressed in Eqs. (5) and (6). Other models add new parameters such as memory access time [16] or tolerable deadline misses [17] while others consider parameters for task allocation in multi-core systems, such as "designated core" [18] or "affinity score" [15], or other application or system-specific parameters. Regarding criticality levels, some models reduce them to two values: low (Lo)—that is, not critical and high (Hi)—that is, critical, while others extend them to n levels of criticality.

Changes were introduced also regarding the way in which computation time is determined for each level and regarding the running modes of the tasks. Computation times are usually determined from the most optimistic value for the lowest criticality mode to the most pessimistic value, which guarantees the highest criticality level of assurance. In MCS task executes in the lowest mode, considering the computation time specific to that mode (optimistic value), if a task having a higher criticality level than the current running mode, exceeds its computation time, and the system switches to a higher running mode, in which lower criticality tasks are either dropped, either scheduled in the remaining processor time, usually in a best-effort manner.

In **Figure 2**, there is an example of a task set, consisting of three mixed-criticality tasks, each having a different criticality level (T1 has a low criticality, T2 medium and T3 high). The system starts in low criticality mode and runs in this mode until time stamp 50, thus considering all the tasks for execution. The systems switches to medium criticality mode at time stamp 50 and runs in this mode until 70, dropping the low criticality task, and then switches in high criticality mode at 70, dropping all other tasks except the high criticality one.

4.2 Scheduling in MCS

Task scheduling refers to the process of determining the order in which various tasks are to be taken up for execution by a system. While traditional scheduling algorithms are focused on throughput and fairness, real-time scheduling algorithms

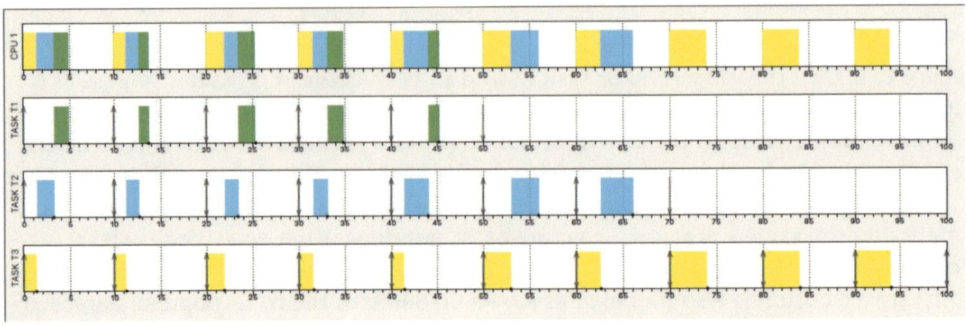

Figure 2.
Example of uniprocessor mixed-criticality task set execution, containing three tasks, each having a different criticality level.

are focused on feasibility (i.e., whether or not it is possible to meet the requirements of all the tasks) and predictability (i.e., the possibility to demonstrate that requirements are met subject to any assumption made) [11].

In multicore systems, the scheduling problem divides into two main sub-problems:

1. Task allocation—each task instance (i.e., job) must be allocated to a core

2. Task scheduling—each task (or job) set allocated to a certain core must be feasible (i.e., schedulable)

In MCS, one must also take into consideration the spacial and time isolation between tasks having different criticality levels. Time isolation is required to ensure that a low criticality task cannot cause a higher criticality task to function incorrectly by taking too much of processor time or by blocking a shared resource, while spacial isolation is required in order to ensure that data used by a task is not altered by other tasks and no tasks will adversely interfere with each other's execution from this point of view [2].

4.2.1 Task allocation

Task allocation in multicore environments is a relatively difficult problem and most of the algorithms used in practice are heuristic [11, 19]. The task-allocation algorithms can be classified into:

- Static—usually done at task level, all tasks are partitioned into subsets, each subset is assigned to a core.

- Dynamic—usually done at job level, each task instance ready for execution is placed in one common priority queue and dispatched to a core for execution, when it becomes available.

Using multicore architectures in MCS brings several advantages regarding the criticality levels temporal isolation issue. Thus, one popular static task-allocation scheme is the one which considers the criticality level of tasks. The first one being proposed by Andreson et al. in Ref. [20]. This schematic divides the task set into subsets of different criticality classes, which are then scheduled to different cores using separate containers for each class, each container having its own local scheduling algorithm.

Other approaches take into consideration, besides the classical utilization factor as defined in Eq. (4), the load balancing [21], resource sharing [22], hardware heterogeneity [15], memory and cache management [23] or energy efficiency [24] or just the schedulability conditions for the task subsets [25].

In MCS task-allocation algorithms, usually make use of classical real-time heuristic methods such as first-fit, next-fit, best-fit or worst-fit [26, 27]:

- First-fit allocates each task to the first core it fits, considering the processor utilization threshold.
- Next-fit allocates each task to the next core it fits, considering the previous task allocation and the processor utilization threshold.
- Best-fit allocates each task to the core that maximizes the utilization factor, using less cores.
- Worst-fit allocates each task to the core that minimizes the utilization factor, giving a better load balance for the cores, compared to the other two approaches.

In the classical heuristics, the cores are selected in ascending order, or descending order of their utilization, based on the heuristics mentioned earlier.

In mixed-criticality systems, these heuristics are adapted in order to take into consideration, besides the utilization factor, one or more of the MC task parameters presented in **Table 1** from Appendix A. For example, Han et al. [28] proposed task-allocation methods based on the task criticality level in conjunction with the worst-fit heuristic and Stângaciu et al. [15] proposed a method based on task affinity in conjunction with the best-fit heuristic. Other papers such as Ortiz et al. [26] proposed their own partitioning methods based on the mixed integer linear programming algorithm. Ren et al. [29] proposed a harmonic partitioning in conjunction with slack time and compared it to all the other classical heuristics mentioned before, while Zhang and Chen [30] proposed a partitioning method called energy-efficient allocating algorithm (EEAA), which is based on the genetic algorithm.

On the other hand, the global scheduling approach makes decisions regarding job assignment to different cores based on feasibility tests by checking sufficient schedulability conditions at runtime [31].

Differences regarding the static and dynamic approaches can be seen in **Figure 3**, where the same task set is allocated to different cores in a multicore system, using (a) a static algorithm and (b) a dynamic one.

The task set consists of five periodic real-time tasks with the following parameters, specified according to Eq. (1):

$$T1 = \{3; 10; 10\}; T2 = \{4; 15; 15\}; T3 = \{7; 10; 10\}; T4 = \{8; 25; 25\}; T5 = \{9; 10; 10\}; \tag{9}$$

In **Figure 3(a)**, the tasks are allocated considering the maximization of the total utilization factor. At the beginning, the total utilization on each core is 0; thus, task $T1$ can be assigned to any of the cores, but it is assigned to the last one, namely CPU 3.

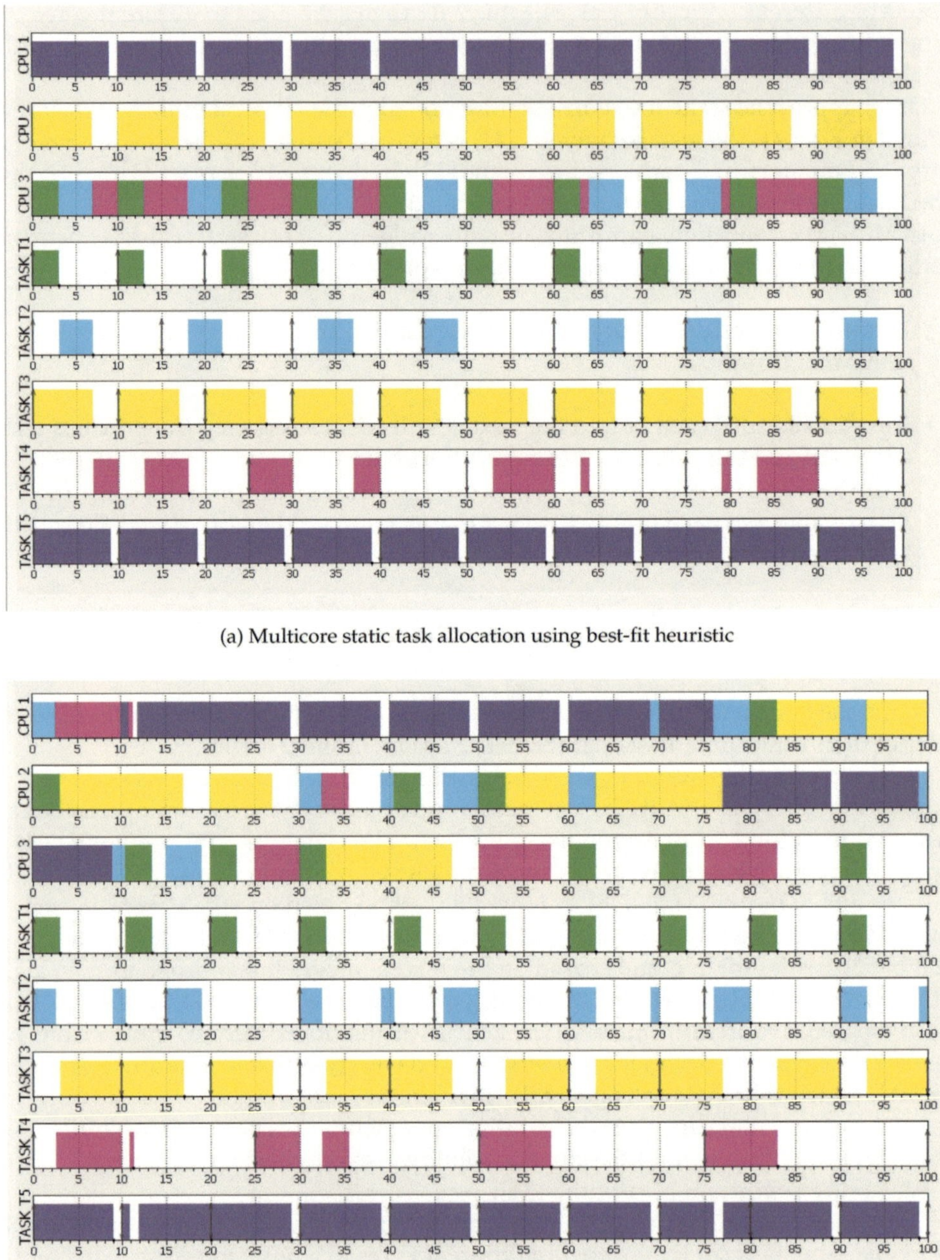

(a) Multicore static task allocation using best-fit heuristic

(b) Multicore dynamic task allocation using a global scheduler

Figure 3.
Examples of multicore task allocation.

Task $T2$ is assigned to the core with the largest utilization factor that can accept task $T2$ without exceeding a total utilization factor of 1 (i.e., 100%), which is CPU 3. Task $T3$ cannot run on the same core, as the total utilization of tasks $T1$, $T2$ and $T3$ would be greater than 1:

$$U_{tot} = \sum_{i=1}^{3} C_i/T_i = 0.3 + 0.2(6) + 0.7 > 1 \tag{10}$$

Thus, task $T3$ is assigned to CPU 2. Because task $T4$ fits to CPU 3 (the core with the highest utilization factor), it is assigned to this core, while the last task is assigned to the only core it fits, namely CPU 1. In this example, this partitioning method provided a total utilization of less than 1, on each core.

In **Figure 3(b)**, there is an example of dynamic task allocation for the same task set as in (a), in which each job is assigned to the core that is able to execute it before its deadline. Thus, unlike the previous example, in this figure, we have tasks that have some jobs executed on a core and other jobs executed on other cores, meaning that this approach supports task migration.

4.2.2 Task scheduling

In a hierarchical multicore architecture, after the task-allocation procedure, a scheduler is responsible for dispatching each task instance according to a predefined algorithm.

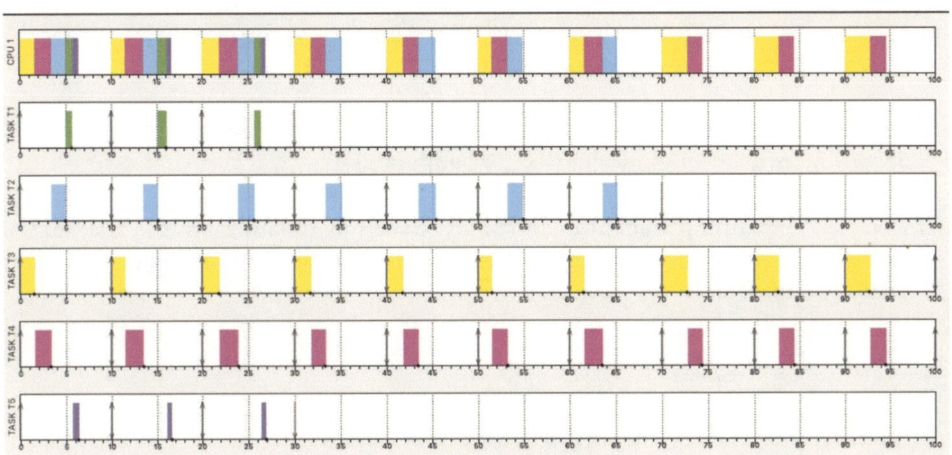

(a) EDF-VD scheduling

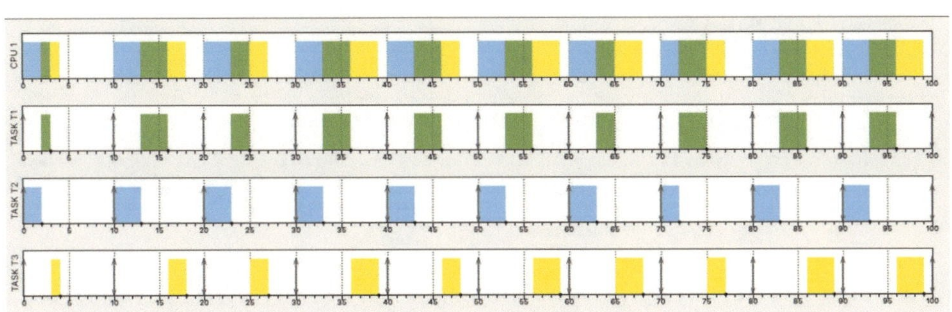

(b) CBEDF scheduling

Figure 4.
Examples of EDF-based MC task scheduling.

The task scheduling is usually done at the core level using classical uniprocessor real-time scheduling algorithms, such as cyclic executives, earliest deadline first (EDF), or fixed priority (FP), specific MCS scheduling methods such as EDF-VD (EDF with virtual deadlines) or CBEDF (criticality based EDF) [4] or hybrid [32]. A comparison between two different approaches at the core level can be seen in **Figure 4**.

Other approaches imply hierarchical scheduling algorithms that contain fixed or dynamic priority servers or containers, each one running a set of tasks or jobs. This approach uses an algorithm for scheduling the containers, while each container can implement its own scheduling algorithm for its allocated tasks [20].

Each real-time scheduling algorithm must provide a schedulability test or a methodology for testing if a task set is schedulable by the algorithm. In the absence of a dedicated schedulability test, one classical method is the response time analysis [33].

5. Methodology for MC task scheduling

In order to implement and schedule an MC application on a multicore system, one can follow the steps depicted in **Figure 5**.

The procedure consists of the following main steps:

1. Develop the applications respecting the real-time programming paradigms, which will result in the task set and its time specifications.

2. Assign a criticality level for each task and determine the MC task parameters according to a selected model (e.g., Vestal's model).

3. Choose a scheduling algorithm and analyze the schedulability of the task set with the selected scheduling algorithm using a schedulability test or the response time analysis approach.

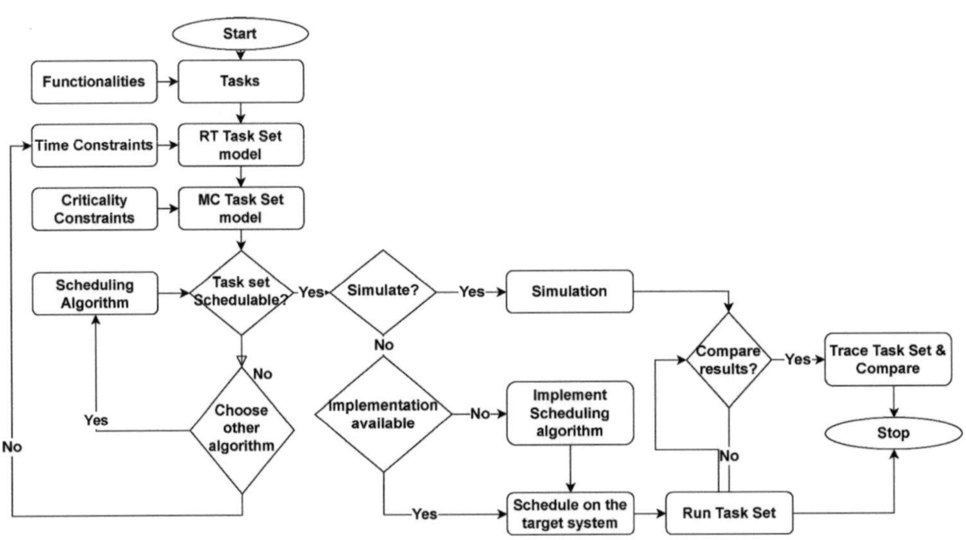

Figure 5.
Example of uniprocessor mixed-criticality task set execution.

4. Optional: schedule the task set, using an implementation of the selected scheduling algorithm on a simulator.

5. Implement the scheduling algorithm (if not already implemented) on your target system.

6. Schedule the application using the scheduling algorithm implementation on your target system.

7. Optional: use a tracing tool or a logic analyzer and compare the task set simulation with the actual application execution.

Different tools developed for RTS, such as aiT from AbsInt, which uses static analysis for task WCET determination and formal verification [34], are still of great use in MCS, especially for high criticality tasks. If we speak about low criticality tasks, tracing and profiling tools such as Percepio Tracelayzer [35] could suffice.

Regarding the development of MC task schedulers, most of the work has been done at the theoretical level. Even if there are numerous MC scheduling methods proposed in the literature [33], there are very few implementations integrated into operating systems. Some of the first to propose a multicore scheduling support implementation for MC tasks were Anderson et al. in Ref. [20]. This approach used an extension of Linux called LITMUS RT [36]. Other proposed implementations for multicore MC tasks using the same LITMUS RT extension followed [37, 38].

Before investing time and effort in implementing a specific scheduling algorithm, running several simulations of that algorithm could be useful. Unfortunately for MCS such simulator are currently missing. Ahmad et al. presented in 2018 [39] the top ten most popular available real-time scheduling simulators with their advantages and disadvantages. One remarkable fact is that none of the existing scheduling simulators has support for mixed-criticality task scheduling. Still, some of them are designed to be customized and extended. Such a simulator is SimSo [14].

Due to the lack of already implemented MC task schedulers in the current operating systems, after analyzing and simulating the algorithms, one must implement them into the running target system. Fortunately, Linux offers since 2024, a new kernel feature called sched-ext [40], which enables the implementation of customized schedulers.

6. Open issues in MC multicore systems

On one hand, most of the development of the MCS has been done from the theoretical point of view regarding execution and scheduling models, schedulability and formal analysis. On the other hand, some progress was made regarding the unification with the practical aspects of real-time systems, with the development of customized scheduling support in Linux. Still, there are some open issues and impediments regarding the large-scale practical implementation of MC systems and its extension to more application fields, especially if we have in mind the complexity of multicore systems:

- lack of simulators—the lack of support for MCS models and scheduling algorithms simulation makes the development of practical applications difficult and slow.

- lack of custom schedulers support in current real-time operating systems—the lack of support for any MC scheduling algorithm in the current operating systems could be at least bypassed by the possibility to develop customizable scheduling algorithms in decent time frame with a medium effort.
- lack of benchmarks for evaluation of MCS—the comparison of different MCS models and scheduling approaches is done mostly at the theoretical level, and the lack of a dedicated set of benchmarks contributes to the slow development of these types of systems.
- lack of tools for real-time monitoring and control—tools for real-time monitoring of the runtime behavior and comparison with the static analysis could also accelerate the development of these systems.

7. Conclusions

Based on its extensions and applicability, the domain of mixed-criticality real-time systems has become very important nowadays. As systems increase more and more in complexity, it is imperative to have the possibility to have tasks with different levels of criticality in the same hardware platform, while protecting the higher criticality tasks from interferences from the lower levels.

The development of deterministic and power-efficient multicore platforms brings advantages in terms of physical and temporal isolation for such systems, but also increases the complexity of the scheduling methods, resulting in further development of this field. As new mixed-criticality task models and schedulers are implemented, the need for better support tools such as simulators and custom scheduling support becomes more stringent.

Thanks

Special thanks to Andrei Briac, who developed an extension of the SimSo simulator for mixed-criticality tasks, which was used to generate some of the examples from this chapter.

Conflict of interest

The author declares no conflict of interest.

Abbreviations

CBEDF	criticality based earliest deadline first
EEAA	energy-efficient allocating algorithm
EDF	earliest deadline first
EDF-VD	earliest deadline first with virtual deadline
FP	fixed priority
IoT	internet of things
RT	real time
RTS	real-time systems
MC	mixed criticality

MCS mixed-criticality systems
WCET worst case execution time

A. Appendix

Reference	Authors	Year	Task/Job Parameters	Crit. levels
[5]	Vestal	2007	C – computation time (vector) T – period (scalar) D – deadline (scalar) L – criticality level (scalar)	4
[41]	Baruah, Li and Stougie	2010	A – release time (scalar) D – deadline (scalar) χ – criticality level (scalar) C – computation time (vector)	2
[42]	Park and Kim	2011	A – release time (scalar) D – deadline (scalar) χ – criticality level (scalar) C – computation time (vector) ES – empty slack (scalar)	2
[43]	Su and Zhu	2013	C – computation time (vector) p – period (scalar) D – deadline (scalar) L – criticality level (scalar) p^{max} – maximum period (scalar) P^{er} – early release points (vector)	2
[44]	Huang et al.	2013	C – computation time (vector) T – minimum inter-arrival (scalar) D – deadline (scalar) L – criticality level (scalar)	n
[45]	Ekberg and Yi	2016	job: e – worst-case execution time (scalar) d – deadline (scalar) μ – mode of the corresponding job type (scalar)	4
[46]	Zhou et al.	2017	T – period (scalar) D – deadline (scalar) N – number of transient faults (scalar) L – criticality level (scalar) C – computation time (vector)	2
[17]	Lee and Shin	2017	C – computation time (vector) T – period (scalar) D – deadline (scalar) L – criticality level (scalar) m – tolerable deadline misses (vector)	n
[16]	Li and He	2017	C – computation time (vector) T – period (scalar) D – deadline (scalar) χ – criticality level (scalar) E – execution time including memory access (vector) M – memory access time (vector)	2

Reference	Authors	Year	Task/Job Parameters	Crit. levels
[47]	Bletsas et al.	2018	C – computation time (vector) T – period (scalar) D – deadline (scalar) k – criticality level (scalar) λ – importance level (scalar)	2
[48]	Wang et al.	2021	task: C – computation time (vector) T – period (scalar) D – deadline (scalar) ζ – criticality level (scalar) V – value of task (vector) job: a – release time (scalar) e – estimated execution (scalar) d – absolute deadline (scalar) f – finish time (scalar)	2
[15]	Stângaciu et al.	2022	C – computation time (vector) T – period (scalar) D – deadline (scalar) L – criticality level (scalar) A – affinity score (scalar)	n
[49]	Zhao et al.	2022	L – criticality level(scalar) T – period (scalar) D – deadline (scalar) C_LO – WCET in LO-crit mode (scalar) C_HI – WCET in HI-crit mode (scalar) st – worst-case stack usage (scalar) p – priority (scalar) γ – preemption threshold (scalar)	2
[18]	Chen et al.	2022	T – period (scalar) D – deadline (scalar) Pri – priority (scalar) m – designated core (scalar) l – criticality level (scalar) C – set of WCETs (vector)	n
[50]	Lesage et al.	2023	T – period (scalar) C – execution time (vector) L – criticality level (scalar) P – priority (scalar) CRP – cache recency profile (scalar)	2

Table 1.
Mixed-criticality task models.

Author details

Cristina-Sorina Stângaciu
Politehnica University Timisoara, Timisoara, Romania

*Address all correspondence to: cristina.stangaciu@cs.upt.ro

References

[1] Ali A, Taj I, Iqbal S, Fayaz M, Khattak AM, Hayat B. Mixed criticality multicore compositional framework. IEEE Access. 2024;**12**:129417-129433

[2] Cerrolaza JP, Obermaisser R, Abella J, Cazorla FJ, Grüttner K, Agirre I, et al. Multi-core devices for safety-critical systems: A survey. ACM Computing Surveys (CSUR). 2020; **53**(4):1-38

[3] Capota EA, Stangaciu CS, Micea MV, Curiac D-I. Towards mixed criticality task scheduling in cyber physical systems: Challenges and perspectives 2007. Journal of Systems and Software. 2019;**156**:204-216

[4] Burns A, Davis RI. A survey of research into mixed criticality systems. ACM Computing Surveys. 2017;**50**(6). DOI: 10.1145/3131347

[5] Vestal S. Preemptive scheduling of multi-criticality systems with varying degrees of execution time assurance. In: 28th IEEE International Real-Time Systems Symposium (RTSS 2007). 2007. pp. 239-243. DOI: 10.1109/RTSS.2007.47

[6] Simó J, Balbastre P, Blanes JF, Poza-Luján J-L, Guasque A. The role of mixed criticality technology in industry 4.0. Electronics. 2021;**10**(3). DOI: 10.3390/electronics10030226

[7] Yao J, Jiahong W, Liu Q, Xiong Z, Zhu G. System-level scheduling of mixed-criticality traffics in avionics networks. IEEE Access. 2016;**4**: 5880-5888

[8] Cinque M, Cotroneo D, De Simone L, Rosiello S. Virtualizing mixed-criticality systems: A survey on industrial trends and issues. Future Generation Computer Systems. 2022;**129**:315-330

[9] Liu CL, Layland JW. Scheduling algorithms for multiprogramming in a hard-real-time environment. Journal of the ACM (JACM). 1973;**20**(1): 46-61

[10] Buttazzo GC. Hard Real-Time Computing Systems: Predictable Scheduling Algorithms and Applications. 2nd ed. United States of America: Springer; 2005. ISBN 0-387-23137-4

[11] Mall R. Real-Time Systems: Theory and Practice. Pearson Education India; 2009. Available from: https://books.google.ro/books?id=coPT7vaEjFsC&dq=mall+real+time+2009&lr=&hl=ro&source=gbs_navlinks_s

[12] Liu JWS. Real-Time Systems. New Jersey: Prentice-Hall; 2000. ISBN 0-13-099651-3

[13] Aloysius Ka-Lau Mok. Fundamental design problems of distributed systems for the hard-real-time environment [PhD thesis]. Massachusetts Institute of Technology; 1983

[14] Chéramy M, Hladik P-E, Déplanche A-M. Simso: A simulation tool to evaluate real-time multiprocessor scheduling algorithms. In: Proceedings of the 5th International Workshop on Analysis Tools and Methodologies for Embedded and Real-Time Systems, WATERS. 2014. Available from: https://hal.science/hal-01052651v1

[15] Stângaciu CS, Capota EA, Stângaciu V, Micea MV, Curiac DI. A hardware-aware application execution model in mixed-criticality internet of things. Mathematics. 2022;**10**(9). DOI: 10.3390/math10091537

[16] Li Z, He S. Fixed-priority scheduling for two-phase mixed-criticality systems.

ACM Transactions on Embedded Computing Systems. 2017;**17**(2). DOI: 10.1145/3105921

[17] Lee J, Shin KG. Development and use of a new task model for cyber-physical systems: A real-time scheduling perspective. Journal of Systems and Software. 2017;**126**:45-56

[18] Chen N, Zhao S, Gray I, Burns A, Ji S, Chang W. Msrp-ft: Reliable resource sharing on multiprocessor mixed-criticality systems. In: 2022 IEEE 28th Real-Time and Embedded Technology and Applications Symposium (RTAS). 2022. pp. 201-213. DOI: 10.1109/RTAS54340.2022.00024

[19] Mascitti A, Cucinotta T, Abeni L. Heuristic partitioning of real-time tasks on multi-processors. In: 2020 IEEE 23rd International Symposium on Real-Time Distributed Computing (ISORC). 2020. pp. 36-42. DOI: 10.1109/ISORC49007.2020.00015

[20] Anderson JH, Baruah SK, Brandenburg BB. Multicore operating-system support for mixed criticality. In: Proceedings of the Workshop on Mixed Criticality: Roadmap to Evolving UAV Certification. Vol. 4. Citeseer; 2009. p. 7. Available from: https://www.cs.unc.edu/~anderson/teach/comp790/papers/2009-anderson-mcws.pdf.

[21] Yang C, Wang H, Zhang J, Zuo L. Semi-partitioned scheduling of mixed-criticality system on multiprocessor platforms. The Journal of Supercomputing. 2022;**78**(5):6386-6410

[22] Zhang Y-W, Ma J-P, Zonghua G. Partitioned scheduling with shared resources on imprecise mixed-criticality multiprocessor systems. IEEE Transactions on Computer-Aided Design of Integrated Circuits and Systems. 2025; **44**(1):65-76

[23] Bakita J, Ahmed S, Osborne SH, Tang S, Chen J, Smith FD, et al. Simultaneous multithreading in mixed-criticality real-time systems. In: 2021 IEEE 27th Real-Time and Embedded Technology and Applications Symposium (RTAS). 2021. pp. 278-291. DOI: 10.1109/RTAS52030.2021.00030

[24] Zhang Y-W, Chen R-K. A survey of energy-aware scheduling in mixed-criticality systems. Journal of Systems Architecture. 2022;**127**:102524

[25] Capota EA, Stangaciu CS, Micea MV, Cretu VI. P_fenp: A Multiprocessor Real-Time Scheduling Algorithm. 2018. DOI: 10.1109/SACI.2018.8440932

[26] Ortiz L, Guasque A, Balbastre P, Simó J. Allocation algorithms for multicore partitioned mixed-criticality real-time systems. Peer Journal of Computer Science. 2024;**10**:e2609

[27] Liu H, Yang M, Wang T, Song C, Zhu S, Chen X. A heuristic mixed real-time task allocation of virtual utilization in multi-core processor. Journal of Information and Intelligence. 2023;**1**(2): 156-177

[28] Han J-J, Tao X, Zhu D, Aydin H, Shao Z, Yang LT. Multicore mixed-criticality systems: Partitioned scheduling and utilization bound. IEEE Transactions on Computer-Aided Design of Integrated Circuits and Systems. 2018; **37**(1):21-34

[29] Ren J, Jun Zhang X, Li WC, Li S, Chu W, Song C. Enhanced harmonic partitioned scheduling of periodic real-time tasks based on slack analysis. Sensors. 2024;**24**(17). DOI: 10.3390/s24175773

[30] Zhang Y-W, Chen R-K. Energy-efficient scheduling of imprecise

mixed-criticality real-time tasks based on genetic algorithm. Journal of Systems Architecture. 2023;**143**:102980

[31] Li H, Baruah S. Outstanding paper award: Global mixed-criticality scheduling on multiprocessors. In: 2012 24th Euromicro Conference on Real-Time Systems. 2012. pp. 166-175. DOI: 10.1109/ECRTS.2012.41

[32] Micea M-V, Stangaciu C-S, Stangaciu V, Curiac D-I. Novel hybrid scheduling technique for sensor nodes with mixed criticality tasks. Sensors. 2017;**17**(7). DOI: 10.3390/s17071504

[33] Burns A, Davis RI. Mixed Criticality Systems - A Review:(13th Edition, February 2022). 2022. This is the 13th version of this review now updated to cover research published up to the end of 2021. Available from: https://eprints.whiterose.ac.uk/183619/

[34] AbsInt Ait. Available from: https://www.absint.com/ait/ [Accessed: January 04, 2025]

[35] Percepio Tracealyzer. Available from: https://percepio.com/tracealyzer/ [Accessed: January 04, 2025]

[36] Calandrino JM, Leontyev H, Block A, Devi UMC, Anderson JH. Litmus rt: A testbed for empirically comparing real-time multiprocessor schedulers. In: 2006 27th IEEE International Real-Time Systems Symposium (RTSS'06). 2006. pp. 111-126. DOI: 10.1109/RTSS.2006.27

[37] Herman JL, Kenna CJ, Mollison MS, Anderson JH, Johnson DM. Rtos support for multicore mixed-criticality systems. In: 2012 IEEE 18th Real Time and Embedded Technology and Applications Symposium. 2012. pp. 197-208. DOI: 10.1109/RTAS.2012.2

[38] Pautet L, Robert T, Tardieu S. Litmus-rt plugins for global static scheduling of mixed criticality systems. Journal of Systems Architecture. 2021; **118**:102221

[39] Ahmad S, Malik S, Kim D-H. Comparative analysis of simulation tools with visualization based on real-time task scheduling algorithms for iot embedded applications. International Journal of Grid and Distributed Computing. 2018;**11**(2):1-10

[40] Sched-ext linux. Available from: https://github.com/sched-ext/scx [Accessed: January 04, 2025]

[41] Baruah S, Li H, Stougie L. Towards the design of certifiable mixed-criticality systems. In: 2010 16th IEEE Real-Time and Embedded Technology and Applications Symposium. 2010. pp. 13-22. DOI: 10.1109/RTAS.2010.10

[42] Park T, Kim S. Dynamic scheduling algorithm and its schedulability analysis for certifiable dual-criticality systems. In: Proceedings of the Ninth ACM International Conference on Embedded Software, EMSOFT'11. New York, NY, USA: Association for Computing Machinery; 2011. pp. 253-262

[43] Hang S, Zhu D. An elastic mixed-criticality task model and its scheduling algorithm. In: Design, Automation and Test in Europe Conference and Exhibition (DATE). *2013*, 2013. pp. 147-152. DOI: 10.7873/DATE.2013.043

[44] Huang P, Kumar P, Stoimenov N, Thiele L. Interference constraint graph—A new specification for mixed-criticality systems. In: 2013 IEEE 18th Conference on Emerging Technologies and Factory Automation (ETFA). 2013. pp. 1-8. DOI: 10.1109/ETFA.2013.6647967

[45] Ekberg P, Yi W. Schedulability analysis of a graph-based task model for mixed-criticality systems. Real-Time Systems. 2016;**52**:1-37

[46] Zhou J, Yin M, Li Z, Cao K, Yan J, Wei T, et al. Fault-tolerant task scheduling for mixed-criticality real-time systems. Journal of Circuits, Systems and Computers. 2017;**26**(01): 1750016

[47] Bletsas K, Awan MA, Souto PF, Akesson B, Burns A, Tovar E. Decoupling criticality and importance in mixed-criticality scheduling. In: Workshop on Mixed Criticality. York; 2018. pp. 25-32. Available from: https://eprints.whiterose.ac.uk/140765/1/WMC_2018_paper_Konst.pdf

[48] Wang W, Mao C, Zhao S, Cao Y, Yi Y, Chen S, et al. A smart semipartitioned real-time scheduling strategy for mixed-criticality systems in 6g-based edge computing. Wireless Communications and Mobile Computing. 2021;**2021**(1):6663199

[49] Zhao Q, Mengfei Q, Huang B, Jiang Z, Zeng H. Schedulability analysis and stack size minimization for adaptive mixed criticality scheduling with semi-clairvoyance and preemption thresholds. Journal of Systems Architecture. 2022; **124**:102383

[50] Lesage B, Dai X, Zhao S, Bate I. Reducing loss of service for mixed-criticality systems through cache-and stress-aware scheduling. In: Proceedings of the 31st International Conference on Real-Time Networks and Systems. 2023. pp. 188-199. DOI: 10.1145/3575757.3593654